To
Joanne!
Good Luck
Good Selling~
Marilyn
Nov/92

CHAMPIONSHIP SELLING
(REVISED REAL ESTATE EDITION)

BY MARILYN JENNINGS

COPYRIGHT 1986
AND 1991 BY: MARILYN C. JENNINGS
P. O. BOX 8425,
STN. "F",
CALGARY, ALBERTA,
CANADA T2J 2V5.

SECOND EDITION: PUBLISHED FEBRUARY 1991

PUBLISHED BY: MCJ PUBLISHING LTD.
P. O. BOX 8425,
STN. "F",
CALGARY, ALBERTA,
CANADA T2J 2V5.

PRINTED IN CANADA BY: EMERSON CLARKE
PRINTING CORPORATION,
9-4001B 19 STREET N.E.,
CALGARY, ALBERTA,
CANADA T2E 6X8.

Canadian Cataloguing in Publication Data

Jennings, Marilyn, 1943-

Championship selling

Rev. real estate ed.
ISBN 0-9695115-0-7

1. Real estate business. 2. Real estate
agents. 3. Real estate agents - Time management.
I. Title.

HD1382.J45 1991   333.33   C91-090119-8

ACKNOWLEDGEMENTS

A very special word of acknowledgement and appreciation to my husband Ed and my daughters Sherri and Shelli for their support, understanding, patience and unlimited assistance along the way.

I say a special "Thank You" to my former Broker/Agent Don Fernie; my present Broker/Agent Rick Baker and his wife Heather; Kevin Clarke; Bev O'Neil; Frank Hickey; Terry Reeder; Suzanne Starrie; Terry Shaw; Peter and Betty Gurr and my Aunt Nola for their time, advice and assistance, which was given cheerfully and freely.

I sincerely acknowledge the contributions of Charles Frank who did much of the editing; Mike and Heather Keller from Keller Art Company Ltd. who did the artwork on the dust cover; Roy White from Roy White Photography for the photo on the dust cover and Jim Heisler, Brian Andersen and all the folks at Emerson Clarke Printing Corporation who had everything to do with the printing. These people made this book a project that was fun to complete.

Last, but by no means least, I gratefully acknowledge the contribution of all those who encouraged me in this endeavour over the years. Encouragement proved to be the ingredient needed to get the project moving again on more than one occasion. My one regret is that my mother, Marion Fagan, who provided loving encouragement throughout all my endeavors, passed away without seeing the end result.

DEDICATION

DEDICATED
TO MY PEERS IN THE REAL ESTATE SALES PROFESSION
IN THE CITY OF CALGARY, ALBERTA, CANADA — THE
FINEST GROUP OF PROFESSIONALS TO BE FOUND
ANYWHERE — WHO HAVE CONTRIBUTED MUCH TO
MY SUCCESS

PREFACE

The one problem that nearly all salespeople have, no

matter what product they are selling, is the problem of getting enough clients to keep them busy. That is especially true in the Real Estate industry! Give any Realtor with an average amount of intelligence and a modicum of personality, a constant supply of loyal, qualified clients and he or she will earn a fortune.

That is a given.

This book presents my "Championship Selling System". When implemented and followed, it will in a short number of years, provide you the Realtor with a continuous and almost limitless supply of prime quality clients — clients who will keep coming back, again and again. In short, it's your ticket to play in the Championship Round.

Understandably, the system works best for Realtors with an already established clientele. Those among you who have been in the business for some time will be able to profit faster and to a greater extent than those who haven't been licensed as long. That does not mean however, that this system is of no benefit to the novice. Quite the contrary. New licensees who follow this system from the beginning of their careers, will become successful in the business far sooner than those who do not. Take my word for it.

In 1985 I earned in excess of $500,000 selling Real Estate in Calgary, Alberta, Canada. I accomplished this following the system outlined in this book. In fact my income has increased every year for the past seven years. During the majority of those years the Real Estate market in Calgary was declining. The fact I was able to improve my performance yearly in a deteriorating market is proof the system works under any circumstances. It's a "Recession Proof" system.

For the past two years my goal has been to increase my income and work less hours. Using the system I've been able to earn in excess of $700,000 working only six months of the year. And I accomplish this without running a single newspaper advertisement, without ever sitting a public open house and I seldom start to work before lunch time.

The Chapters that follow detail a system that will enable you to be as successful as you want to be in the Real Estate Profession — The Greatest Profession In The Whole World.

Good Reading and Good Selling!

Marilyn Jennings,

P.O. Box 8425, Stn. "F",
Calgary, Alberta,
Canada T2J 2V5.

TABLE
OF
CONTENTS

SECTION ONE

A SYSTEM FOR "CHAMPIONSHIP" REALTORS

CHAPTER 1   21
Greatest Profession In The Whole World
Reasons For Failure Are Many

CHAPTER 2   25
The "Championship Selling System"
Systems Give Life To Plans

CHAPTER 3   29
Get Control Of Your Time
The Sea Captain Story

CHAPTER 4   33
Upgrade Your Clientele
Prospect Categories

CHAPTER 5   37
A Profound Statement
An "ABOVE AVERAGE" Goal
So You'd Like To Get Lucky

SECTION TWO

AN EFFECTIVE CLIENT RETENTION PROGRAM

CHAPTER 6   45
Client Retention Program — What Does It Mean?
Definition And Example
Share Success With Clients
Promotions Should Have Classy Touch

CHAPTER 7   49
Building Our Business With Repeats

SECTION THREE

AN ACTIVE REFERRAL SYSTEM

CHAPTER 8   53
Two Sources Of Referrals
Private Referrals
Realtor Referrals

CHAPTER 9   57
They Need To Buy
Source Of Additional Clients

CHAPTER 10   61
Developing A Realtor Referral Network
Size Of Community Is Irrelevant
Use Personal Contact
Use The Mails
Always Be Referral Conscious

CHAPTER 11   67
Get A System In Place

SECTION FOUR

TIME MANAGEMENT

CHAPTER 12   73
Time Management — What Is It?
Delegate The Unproductive
What Is My Time Worth
Improve Your "Quality of Life"

CHAPTER 13   77
The Initial Client Interview
Purpose Of Initial Client Interview
The Client Interview Step By Step
Very Effective Time Management Tool
People Happy To Wait For Interview

CHAPTER 14   95
The Rating System For Showing Property
Play The Name And Rate Game
Time For A Second Look

CHAPTER 15   99
Certifying Cheques
Putting Up Signs

CHAPTER 16   103
Beware Negative Non Achievers
No Reflection On Management

CHAPTER 17   109
When A Contract Is Signed Call Up The Reserves
Two Types Of Contract

CHAPTER 18   113
Mortgaging — The Time Saving Way
Get Yourself A Good Broker
Why A Broker?
Broker Fees — Who Pays?
Objective — Do Income Generating Activity
Let The Broker Do The Leg Work
Some Do's And Some Don'ts
Don't Lose Your Objectivity
Going Quotes Aren't Going Rates
Penalties For Early Pay-out

CHAPTER 19   123
Listings And Time Management
Forget Selling — Become A Good Lister!
Most Common Vendor/Seller Complaint
Two Easy Solutions
Train Your Vendor/Seller To Call You
Sell Your Listings To Other Realtors
A Vendor's/Seller's Mortal Sin
What! No Calls? Is The Price Too High?
Second Most Common Vendor/Seller Complaint
Don't Make Promises
List For Long Term And Cancel Anytime
Concentrate On Pricing Right
Over Priced Listings Earn Big Commissions
Never Cut Your Commission
Play Business Card Poker

CHAPTER 20   141
Servicing Listings
Keep Paperwork At A Minimum
Promote Your Listings At Realtor Open Houses
Distribute Flyers To Real Estate Offices
Make Showings Easy For Other Realtors

CHAPTER 21   147
How Many Listings Should A Realtor Carry?
Guarantee Yourself Any Income You Want

CHAPTER 22   151
Technological Advancements
Get Yourself Computerized Now
Instantaneous Information
A Program For The Realtor In The Field
The Fax Revolution
A Coincidental Illustration

CHAPTER 23   159
Hiring An Assistant
When You Hit The "Time Barrier" Hire An Assistant
Basic Income Producing Activities
An Assistant Not A Secretary
Remuneration, Qualities And Job Description

CHAPTER 24   165
Assistants' Duties
Listing Presentations
Servicing Listings
Property Showings
Accepted Offers
Transaction Closings
Telephone Calls
Computer In-puts And Print-outs
Another Perspective

CHAPTER 25   173
My Job Description: By Suzanne Starrie
Preparation Of Documentation
Processing Listings
Post-listing Services
Processing Offers
Setting Up Appointments
Maintaining Communications
The Key To Efficient Operation
Office Management
A Car Is Essential
Take Off The Pressure

CHAPTER 26   185
Hiring A Driver
Two Good Reasons For Hiring A Driver
Clients And Needs Get More Attention

CHAPTER 27   191
My Job Description: By Terry Shaw
Vehicle Operation
Realtor Assistance
Miscellaneous Tasks
Apportionment Of Time

CHAPTER 28   197
You Need All The Essential Tools
Don't Misuse The Essential Tools

CHAPTER 29   201
The Value Of Leisure Time
Exclude Non-essential Activities

CHAPTER 30   205
Personal Promotion
Promote Yourself — Don't Advertise Property
Personalize Everything
Tell Your Clients, The Press And Your Peers
Go First Class And Be Consistent
Some Examples

CHAPTER 31   231
Closing Thoughts

SECTION ONE

A SYSTEM FOR "CHAMPIONSHIP" REALTORS

" C H A P T E R   1 "

GREATEST PROFESSION
IN THE WHOLE WORLD

There isn't another profession in the whole world

that allows a mere human to excel like the Real Estate business does. What other calling in life rewards effort so lavishly? There isn't another profession in which members experience the thrill of psychological and financial fulfillment, to such a satisfying degree.

Our Real Estate licence gives us access to a vast warehouse of merchandise. That warehouse remains stocked with multi-million dollar inventories — the properties listed for sale in our marketing areas.

Our licence also gives us a "CONTINUING" interest of somewhere between 0% and 100% (commission) in every piece of Real Estate in the jurisdiction that granted our licence. All we have to do is convince our Partners (Vendors/Sellers) to list their property for sale so we can get our money (commissions) out.

No matter how many times the property sells, our interest continues! We get all this for an investment of only a few hundred dollars. No other licence affords more opportunity to the recipient for so little.

Yet, year after year, thousands of people enter the Real Estate business and fail.

REASONS FOR
FAILURE ARE MANY

There are many reasons why people enter the Real Estate business and fail. Companies hire people and don't train them properly. The industry as a whole, does little to teach people how to sell. People come into the business with the impression they can make a fast buck. Most companies do little to discourage that motivation.

New Salespeople are seldom told, that this is not a "Get Rich Quick" business. They are not told they'll have to work long, hard hours for several years in order to make it big; that they shouldn't enter this business unless they plan to make a career of it; that it takes several years to build up a clientele; and they should have sufficient financial reserves to get through the first twelve months. Sales Managers hire people who only want part-time work, get them licensed, and hope they'll become full-time Salespeople.

All of the foregoing plus numerous other misconceptions, contribute greatly to the failure rate of Real Estate licensees. But, the purpose of this book is not to analyze and deal with the reasons for failure. That would fill a book on its own. No, the purpose of this book is to present a system that is tried and proven and has made the writer very successful. If followed closely, this system will help anyone who has chosen Real Estate Sales as a lifetime career, become more successful.

So, if you are a part-timer seeking an extra buck, or a short-timer seeking a fast buck, this book is not for you. The system, outlined in the Chapters to come, is premised on a commitment to hard work over an extended period of time. It won't, and I repeat, won't work on a hit and miss basis. On the other hand, the longer it is applied the more productive are the results.

"CHAPTER 2"

THE "CHAMPIONSHIP SELLING SYSTEM"

I call my system "The Championship Selling System".

It is composed of three distinct elements or parts. These elements are:

1) An Effective Client Retention Program;
2) An Active Referral System;
3) Good Efficient Time Management.

Each element is as important to the system as the other. Without any one of them the system wouldn't be effective at all. Combined properly to form the "Championship Selling System" they provide one of the most powerful, productive selling systems ever devised.

SYSTEMS GIVE
LIFE TO PLANS

It's no secret that in order to be successful we must have a financial goal or objective to aim for. We also know that to reach our goal, we have to have a plan that we can follow to get us there. The dictionary defines the word **"plan"**, as it applies in this case, as **"a method or way of proceeding (that is or has been) thought out in advance"**. I.E. **"It all went according to plan"**; or **"A map, sketch or layout to be followed"**.

A system, on the other hand, is defined as **"a set of connected things or parts that form a whole or work together"**. A plan then, is an outline of how you are going to achieve an end result. A system is much more comprehensive. It connects all the parts of a plan so they work together as a whole.

Systems give life to plans! For example, your plan to reach your goal may outline among other things, that you need two listings per week plus two sales. Following the right system — **"The Championship Selling System"** — will ensure that you get them.

That's why every salesperson needs a system! To bring their plans to life!!

One salesperson who has adopted my system calls it an "Insurance Policy Against Being Average". Now, you too can have that insurance.

" C H A P T E R   3 "

GET CONTROL
OF YOUR TIME

One of the most common reasons for Realtors not

doing better is they are not in control of their time.

I know. That used to be my problem too. I was doing time consuming menial tasks that should have been delegated to others. I was also wasting valuable hours doing things the wrong way and at the wrong time.

Sound familiar? If it does, then this is the book for you!

The better management of your time is a recurring theme in this book. It can't be said too often: **"Good Effective Time Management" Is Absolutely Essential To Success In The Real Estate Sales Profession!**

THE SEA
CAPTAIN STORY

Someone once asked the Captain of a sea going vessel if he could take a party to any navigable point in the world, accessible by or from an ocean. His answer was: "Yes, provided you can tell me two things. First, can you tell me where you want to go? Second, can you tell me exactly where you are right now? Based on that information and using my records, charts, graphs, and other tools of my trade, I can plot a course to take you there. But, if you don't know where you are right now, it's impossible for me to take you where you want to go."

In his answer, that salty old Sea Captain paraphrased one of the key ideas in Time Management. "If you want to achieve a desired result, you have to know where you currently are." In other words, before the better management of your time can have any significance you must have a goal. But even more important, you must always know exactly where you are on the way to achieving that goal.

As we journey through this book, perhaps you too will decide to become a Sea Captain, take control of your own vessel, plot a course to where you want to go, and implement a system that will take you to your goal.

" C H A P T E R 4 "

UPGRADE YOUR
CLIENTELE

Realtors fail to EXCEL for many reasons, but among

the most common is that they work tirelessly to attract the "poorest" quality prospects.

I had that problem too. Like most people in the business, I spent my promotional efforts and a goodly portion of my budget, trying to attract the wrong type of prospect. As a result, I found myself working with a poor quality clientele. That meant I was working much harder than I had to. Consequently, I was earning far less than I should have been.

On the surface, there appears to be little relationship between upgrading your clientele, time management and one's earnings. But really, there is. Think about it as we proceed through the pages to come. The significance of that relationship will become quite clear.

PROSPECT
CATEGORIES

The best prospect is the client who has already dealt with you. The second best, is the one referred to you by a client who has dealt with you previously. The third best, is one referred to you by another trusted professional or friend, such as your Lawyer, Accountant, Banker, etc. The fourth best, is one referred to you by someone in your business from another town, who has a client moving to your area. (e.g. The prospect moving from Calgary to Your Town, and referred to you by their Calgary Realtor).

The poorest quality prospect is the one who calls on a newspaper ad. Think about it! Where do AVERAGE

Realtors get their clients from? From newspaper ads!! When I was satisfied with being AVERAGE, that's where I too found the majority of my clients. I was out there competing with all the other AVERAGE Realtors for my share of the poorest group of prospects!

It's no wonder my earnings were nothing to crow about!

I got out of that competition the day I decided to be ABOVE AVERAGE. I quit advertising properties in the newspaper eleven years ago. Yet, my income is now more than 20 times higher than it was then.

All of my promotional efforts and budget have been redirected to the four best categories of prospects. The four referred to above. Over 85% of my business comes from these sources. The balance comes from sign calls and neighbourhood canvasses.

" C H A P T E R   5 "

A PROFOUND
STATEMENT

The first step toward becoming truly successful in this

business is to determine where you are right now, and then set **ABOVE AVERAGE** goals. In order to do that, it is necessary to do as I did several years ago. What prompted me to completely re-assess my "**Methods Of Operating**" was a rather profound statement I once read in a magazine article. It said, "**If you want to be AVERAGE, do what everyone else in your business does. If you want to be ABOVE AVERAGE, do the opposite**".

After pondering this statement for a while, I came to realize that the collective goal of North American society is to make everyone AVERAGE. All our institutions cater to the AVERAGE person. Institutionally the Real Estate Profession does the same as all the others.

The more I thought about it, the more I realized just how AVERAGE I had been for the first 14 years of my career. In fact, I did all the things AVERAGE Realtors did! Like all the others, the reasons I gave to justify being AVERAGE were really only excuses for not being more successful.

AN "ABOVE AVERAGE" GOAL

After 14 years of being AVERAGE, I decided it was time to be the best. I immediately set as my goal, "That in five years — 1984 — I would be the #1 MLS Realtor for the Calgary Real Estate Board".

In a sense, when one decides to be ABOVE AVERAGE it's a decision to break with society. Having just moved to Calgary from over 2000 miles away, nearly everyone thought I was nuts. They were trained by AVERAGE Managers to think, act, work, and set goals like AVERAGE Realtors. That's why they couldn't relate to my goal. It was way ABOVE AVERAGE with rewards that were beyond their comprehension.

Reaching that goal meant I had to increase my annual income by more than 10 times. It meant becoming one of the Top Earners in the Real Estate business Nationally and Internationally. It also meant I would be recognized in my industry and the sales field in general as a Success Story. I would be called on to address meetings, seminars and sit on Top Producers panels.

Needless to say, I reached my goal by a comfortable margin over my nearest competitor. I had completed a long and very rewarding journey — the journey from being AVERAGE to being ABOVE AVERAGE! It was five years earlier, however, that I had taken the first step.

You can take the first step right now by setting an ABOVE AVERAGE goal for yourself. **Remember, you can never be ABOVE AVERAGE as long as you pursue AVERAGE goals!!**

SO YOU'D LIKE
TO GET LUCKY!

When you're working to realize a goal, you'll find that in the process you always achieve other accomplishments you never intended or expected to. Often, these additional accomplishments have a far more significant impact on your own life, and the lives of others, than the attainment of the original goal you were striving to achieve. In every case, when I've achieved a goal this has been the case. That's what makes setting goals and achieving them so interesting — you always accomplish far more than you originally intended to.

For instance, in 1985 my goal was to be among the top five Realtors for Re/max internationally. I ended up being #4. Without realizing it at the time, this was good enough to make me the #1 female Realtor in the Re/max international system. Being the #1 female Realtor in the Re/max system for that year wasn't my original goal, but that result, which came about because I achieved my original goal attracted the most interest by far. It brought me considerable international recognition and notoriety including interviews in several publications, radio and television appearances, and a whole string of paid speaking engagements that have taken me the length and breadth of the continent.

To a greater or lesser extent the same thing happens to everyone who achieves a goal they've set for themselves. And this isn't a phenomenon that's unique to the sales profession. Apparently a few years ago a fellow — named Alexander Graham Bell — had a wife who had a serious hearing problem. While working to invent a hearing aid for his deaf wife he invented another gadget called the telephone. You see Bell was working to realize a certain goal, and in the process achieved an accomplishment that had a far more significant impact on the world than the hearing aid he was working on for his deaf wife.

Many people hear that story and conclude that Bell was lucky. They miss the point completely. You see, there's an important lesson in all of this. It's really quite simple. IF YOU HAVE GOALS AND YOU WORK HARD TO ACHIEVE THEM — YOU'RE GOING TO GET LUCKY!! Or to put it another way, "LUCK IS A BY-PRODUCT OF ACHIEVING A GOAL!!

How lucky — do you — want to be?

SECTION TWO:

AN EFFECTIVE CLIENT
RETENTION PROGRAM

"CHAPTER 6"

CLIENT RETENTION PROGRAM — WHAT DOES IT MEAN?

We're living in a very sophisticated society. It's a

society where statistical information is available or can be developed readily, regarding just about everything we do. Almost every like, dislike and habit of virtually every group of people, has been tabulated at one time or another, by either a private or government sponsored polling organization. Having all this information available allows us, today more than ever before, to turn the habits of people to our own economic advantage. Witness the following example. It applies directly to you and I.

Real Estate statistics for Canada and the United States tell us that people re-purchase, on average, every 2 1/2 to 3 years. Note that we said people re-purchase — not that they sell or move. We know some do sell and move. Others simply purchase some additional Real Estate for themselves, their family, their company, etc.

This means that your previous clients re-purchase every 2 1/2 to 3 years. These are the absolute best prospects in the world — people who have already dealt with you! Doesn't it make good sense then to spend a hefty portion of your promotional budget to retain them as clients? Of course it does!! That's why every Realtor needs "**An Effective Client Retention Program**".

DEFINITION
AND EXAMPLE

Let's define "An Effective Client Retention Program". Basically we are talking about, "**Any program of regular contact with former clients, that ensures they deal**

with you AND ONLY YOU, when they decide to re-purchase the product you sell.''

To ensure this happens, I do two major promotions yearly. Both have a twofold purpose. First, they're aimed at retaining my clientele. Second, they keep my referral system active. We'll talk more about the referral system later.

At Christmas time, I give all my past and present clients a Champagne Kit. It contains a bottle of bubbly, two candles, two candle holders, two glasses, an ice bucket, and a book of matches. In early June, I give them a bar-b-que apron. It's monogrammed with my signature, phone number, and my company logo.

These are accompanied by a letter, thanking them for their referrals and soliciting more referrals. I tell them how well I am doing in a way that allows them to share in my success. In other words I brag! But in a nice way!!

SHARE SUCCESS
WITH CLIENTS

People love to share and participate in exciting events. However, outside of Political Campaigns they are seldom given an opportunity to share in making someone else successful. Give your clients the opportunity to contribute to your success and you'll be amazed at how eagerly they respond.

After both these promotions, I am literally flooded with business. I hear from many clients whom I haven't heard from in months. Without exception, they're proud of the contribution they make to my success. Whenever you can, give your clients the opportunity to say, **"Hey, I helped make him or her successful, and they still remember me for it!"**

PROMOTIONS SHOULD HAVE CLASSY TOUCH

The type of promotion you choose to do isn't nearly as important as the way it's done. So, whatever the type of promotion, do it with class. Convey the impression that you care about your promotion and the recipient. Too often, an otherwise excellent promotion proves ineffective, because it's presented in a haphazard way. It takes only a few extra pennies to have a gift prepared properly.

Of course it helps if your promotions are unique. People like to receive gifts, cards or whatever, that are novel, different and useful. The giver is more apt to be remembered if gifts have these characteristics about them.

One automobile salesperson I know has pumpkins delivered to all his clients just before Halloween. He gets fantastic results from this promotion. An insurance salesperson has a basket of Easter Eggs delivered to his clients at Easter time. Obviously there is no shortage of unique ideas. Regardless of what promotion you decide on, be sure to make it first class.

" C H A P T E R   7 "

BUILDING OUR
BUSINESS WITH REPEATS

Always remember that being Commission Salespeople

we're in business for ourselves. Like all other business people we have to be concerned about building our business. In 1989, I had 204 client transactions and 83 of them were repeats. Those were 83 easy transactions. In case you're wondering, 83 is about four times as many transactions, as the AVERAGE SUCCESSFUL NORTH AMERICAN REALTOR has in a whole year.

Far more important, is the fact that my repeats will keep growing year by year. The day is fast approaching when I can look forward to over 100 transactions yearly strictly from repeats.

The following chart is based on an increase of only 25 new clients per year. It illustrates the potential sales available to a Realtor, if only 1/5 of his previous clients re-purchase from him in 2 1/2 to 3 year cycles. The amount of income available from this source is beyond belief.

YEAR	NEW CLIENTS				TOTAL
1	25				25
2	25				25
3	25				25
4	25	+ 5 RPTS FR YR 1			30
5	25	+ 5 RPTS FR YR 1	+ 5 RPTS FR YR 2		35
6	25	+ 5 RPTS FR YR 1	+ 5 RPTS FR YR 2	+ 5 RPTS FR YR 3	40

An "Effective Client Retention Program" will build your business and upgrade the quality of your clientele, because it is aimed at retaining for you, the best quality prospect in the whole world — the client who has previously dealt with you!

SECTION THREE

AN ACTIVE REFERRAL SYSTEM

" CHAPTER 8 "

TWO SOURCES
OF REFERRALS

Broadly speaking there are two sources of referral

clients we can cultivate. First, there are those generated by "Previous Clients" and people in "Positions of Influence" who refer friends, relatives, acquaintances and their own clients to us. I call these "Private Referrals". Secondly, there are those generated by "Realtors" in other communities in Canada, the United States and elsewhere in the world. I refer to these as "Realtor Referrals". Included in this latter category are clients I refer to Realtors in other communities and countries.

PRIVATE REFERRALS

Every time I complete a transaction I recruit a new member to my "Sales Force". I make sure that everyone I deal with understands that I expect them to promote my cause. I rely on them to keep me busy. They're given my Personal Brochures to display in their office or place of business. I get as much commitment from them as possible.

I inform each of them I don't pay for leads. After all, they wouldn't feel very good about their friend having referred them to me, if he was getting paid for doing so.

In addition, I recruit people to my referral team who are not clients, but who are in "Positions of Influence". I'm talking about people such as Bankers, Insurance Agents, Service Station Operators, Lawyers, etc. I make sure these people always have a supply of brochures to give to clients and associates.

Now, all Sales Forces deserve a pat on the back once in a while, and on occasion a little reminder they may not be performing up to par. My two annual promotions accompanied by my letter accomplish both these objectives.

I keep a "Family Tree" type of record for each client. When the tree stops growing I fertilize it. A phone call to the roots or one of the branches often results in a remarkable spurt of new healthy growth.

REALTOR
REFERRALS

It's no secret that ours is a very mobile society. People move North to South, East to West, city to city, city to country, country to country, and vice-versa almost at whim. In addition to getting referrals from the two sources previously mentioned, a large portion of my referral transactions, are with clients who've been referred to me by Realtors in other communities across Canada and the U.S.A.. This doesn't happen by accident!

Since many long distance moves take place in the summer, in the early spring of each year I send a letter with one of my Personal Brochures to every Re/Max Realtor across Canada, to several hundred Realtors not connected with Re/Max in various parts of Canada, and to Re/Max Realtors in selected areas of the United States — about 12,000 Realtors in all.

This network keeps growing year by year. As well as getting clients from other Realtors, I refer clients to Realtors in the new locations they move to. I then receive a Referral Fee when they purchase a home in their new town or city.

Quite often, Realtor referred clients are people who are transferred from one community to another by their company. All Realtor referred clients are prime prospects because you've been recommended to them by their Realtor whom they know and trust.

" C H A P T E R 9 "

THEY NEED
TO BUY!

Company Transferred Employees are usually better

prospects than those who are relocating on their own. In many cases they "**Need to Buy**". Many companies provide added company benefits to transferred employees who purchase a home in their new city.

The costs associated with selling their present home are usually paid by their employer. Companies normally pay moving expenses. Costs associated with the purchase of a home in their new city are looked after too. Many companies provide additional perks: Broadloom or carpet allowances; housing cost differentials; interest subsidies; low interest and interest free mortgages are the more common additional benefits.

Still other companies give their employees housing guarantees when transferring them. Other employers pay the carrying costs incurred by the employee until the home is sold and in addition pay the basic selling costs such as Real Estate commission and legal fees. Because of the perks associated with moving, Company Transferred Employees will often have more money available to spend on housing in their new city than others selling similar homes and moving from the same area.

To further assist transferred employees, companies often pick up all or part of any loss where home values have declined. For us Realtors, this means that Company Transferred Employees are prime, prime prospects. They often "**Need to Buy**" to take advantage of added company benefits.

SOURCE OF
<u>ADDITIONAL CLIENTS</u>

Company Transferred Employees make great clients for yet another reason. They know others from their company who are following them to your city in the near future and later on. They can recommend you to their fellow employees, who are following.

On one occasion a few years ago, a Company Transferred Employee was referred to me by their Realtor. I sold them a home. Over the next year I sold homes to 17 other employees transferred by the same company. An entire department relocated from one city to another. In spite of the fact a company other than the one I work for handled the sales of their homes in their former community, I sold every employee.

Remember these points all apply to clients of yours who are being transferred by their companies to other cities as well.

" C H A P T E R   10 "

DEVELOPING A REALTOR
REFERRAL NETWORK

An obvious part of any **"Active Referral System"**

must be a Realtor network. Such a network will not develop on its own. Developing one requires hard work and detailed planning.

I suggest you start with your own Province or State. Basically, you want to set up an exchange system, whereby you exchange clients with Realtors from other towns and cities. When they send you a client, you pay them a 25% referral fee when the transaction closes. When you send them a client, they pay you on the same basis.

SIZE OF COMMUNITY IS IRRELEVANT

During 25 years in the profession, I've sold Real Estate in virtually every size of community. There really isn't any difference between one community and another, when it comes to developing Realtor to Realtor referral business, except in terms of volume. Even small rural centres have some movement of people.

When people move from one community to another, a Realtor in the community left behind should earn a Referral Fee. Unless of course he or she is asleep at the switch. All one need do is contact a Realtor in the community to which the client is moving. Make the appropriate referral fee arrangements and arrange for the client to meet the Realtor on arrival. It's that simple.

In recent years I've had clients referred to me by Realtors from small rural centres in other provinces, from large cities and everything in between. As well, I've referred clients to Realtors from both small and large communities in Canada and the United States.

Many smaller communities, especially in the North, are Company Towns. Some companies rotate employees in and out of these towns regularly. For the past several years, I've had a regular exchange program in place with a Realtor from one small town in the north. We've exchanged clients regularly as a small resource company working near the community moved their employees to and from different locations. Both of us have profited from this arrangement. I'm certain it will continue for years to come.

USE PERSONAL CONTACT

The best method of developing your Realtor network is by personal contact. A visit to the local Real Estate office when you are in a particular town on holidays or other business, will often pay handsome dividends.

One year on a short holiday trip to Victoria, British Columbia, I dropped in on a local Realtor who was hosting a public Open House on a Sunday afternoon. I left some of my Personal Brochures with the Realtor. In turn they were passed along to another Realtor in his office whose sister and husband lived in Calgary. She referred them to me when they wanted to list their home. I listed it, sold it for them and sold them another home.

Since then they've referred their friends to me. I've listed their friends home, sold it for them and sold them another. These people have since referred other acquaintances to me. I expect to do business with all these people again and with their friends as well.

Personal contact can also be made with other Realtors by attending conventions, conferences and workshops, sponsored by your provincial or state associations or boards. If your company is provincial, state-wide, or national in scope, you can develop your network internally to a large degree. Personal contact can be made at internal company conferences.

USE THE
MAILS

One of the more effective ways of expanding a Realtor network is to use the mails. Sending promotional material accompanied by introductory letters, to all Realtors or selected Realtors in specific communities, has paid handsome dividends for me. Judging from the number of pieces of mail I receive from Realtors from other communities, it must also pay dividends for others. I've found that a carefully planned well-timed annual mail campaign, where I added new territory each year, is the most effective way of expanding my network.

ALWAYS BE
REFERRAL CONSCIOUS

If you simply ask each client who's leaving your area, if they'd like you to arrange contact with a good Realtor in the community they're moving to, you could increase your annual income by several hundreds to several thousands of dollars.

What's involved? Simply call an active Real Estate office in the area. Ask for the Owner or Manager. Tell them you want to speak with their best Residential Realtor or Commercial Realtor, depending on your clients needs. If your client prefers a male or a female ask for their best male or female Realtor.

When you speak with the Realtor, ask if he or she is working referrals with anyone else from your city. If the answer is no, proceed. If the answer is yes, ask for the next best Realtor who isn't. The reason? You want an arrangement that's reciprocal. You want the person to whom you refer your clients, to send all their referral clients to you in return. If they're already working referrals with someone from your city the best you're going to get is part of their return referral business. And the objective is to get it all!

Finally, make a crystal clear Referral Fee arrangement with them so there'll be no misunderstanding. Give him or her your client's name(s) and phone number(s). Follow up on your verbal arrangement with a written one. Include any material that will help them conclude a sale. You stand to earn a referral fee of anywhere from a few hundred to over a thousand dollars for a minimum of both effort and time.

When realtors exchange referrals with each other, everyone involved in the process wins. Clients benefit, because they're introduced to a competent professional in their new locale. The referring realtor benefits by receiving a referral fee. And the realtor in the town or city where the client is moving to obtains a loyal client as well as a virtually guaranteed commission.

Always remember, referrals pay big dividends to both the sender and the recipient!

" C H A P T E R   11 "

GET A SYSTEM
IN PLACE

If you don't have "**An Active Referral System**" in

place, do something about it pronto! You're missing some easy deals with some of the best quality prospects you could possibly hope to deal with.

Like an "Effective Client Retention Program" an "Active Referral System" builds your business and upgrades the quality of your clientele, because it is aimed at the three next best categories of prospects.

Earlier I mentioned that in 1989 I had 83 repeat client transactions. In other years I've had as many as 94 repeat client transactions. The number varies slightly from year to year depending on market conditions. But the day is fast approaching when I can look forward to over 100 transactions yearly strictly from repeats. In 1989 I also had 88 transactions that were referrals. This number keeps growing annually as well! Let's put it another way. I'm looking forward to some pretty fantastic years!!

Previously, we noted that statistics show clients repurchase every 2 1/2 to 3 years. Unlike "Repeats" you can begin reaping rewards from "Referrals" immediately. The chart at the end of Chapter 7 would approximate the one below if only 8% of a Realtor's clients produced one referral per year with whom a transaction was concluded.

YEAR	NEW CLIENTS					TOTAL
1	25	+	2 REFS YR 1			27
2	25	+	4 REFS YR 2			29
3	25	+	7 REFS YR 3			32
4	25	+	10 REFS YR 4	+ 5 RPTS FR YR 1		40
5	25	+	14 REFS YR 5	+ 5 RPTS FR YR 1	+ 5 RPTS FR YR 2	49

Worked faithfully, **"An Effective Client Retention Program"** together with **"An Active Referral System"**, can provide a Salesperson in any field with an almost limitless supply of clients after a short number of years. At the same time the quality of clientele he or she works with will be continually upgraded.

Blend the above ingredients with techniques for "Good Effective Time Management" found in the next section. You'll be well on the way to achieving a degree of success in the Real Estate Profession that you may never have dreamed possible.

SECTION FOUR

TIME MANAGEMENT

" C H A P T E R   12 "

TIME MANAGEMENT —
WHAT IS IT?

Simply upgrading the type of prospect you work with

is a giant step, toward using your time more efficiently. **Time management is both the "Efficient" and "Effective" use of one's time to achieve a goal.**

Squeezing more sales calls into a given period of time, might on the surface appear to be more "Efficient". However, if the number of sales fail to increase, because you are rushing your presentation, then such a tactic is not "Effective".

What we have to strive for in the management of our time is a proper balance. One that will make us both "Efficient" and "Effective". I had that very problem. I was spending my time both "Inefficiently" and "Ineffectively".

DELEGATE THE UNPRODUCTIVE

Today I spend my time doing only those things, which are direct income producing activities, plus those things which because of licensing regulations I can not delegate to others.

I suggest you take a look over the next several days at each task you are about to perform. Ask yourself, **"Will the task I am about to complete result in producing more income for me?"** If it won't it should be delegated. Or perhaps it shouldn't be done at all.

The following is a good rule of thumb for determining if a job should be delegated or not. First, determine how much you want to earn in a year. Second, decide how many hours you're going to work to earn it. Third, divide the number of hours into what you're going to earn, to find out how much you're worth per hour. If the task can be performed by someone else for less per hour it should be delegated, unless there is a compelling reason why it shouldn't be. The important thing is, that exceptions to the delegation rule should be few and far between.

WHAT IS YOUR TIME WORTH

Why not determine the hourly value of your time right now? Just apply the above formula to the chart below.

MY GOAL	+	BUSINESS EXPENSES	=	GROSS INCOME	÷	WORK HOURS	=	HOURLY VALUE
$ 50,000		_____		_____		_____		_____
$ 60,000		_____		_____		_____		_____
$ 70,000		_____		_____		_____		_____
$ 80,000		_____		_____		_____		_____
$ 90,000		_____		_____		_____		_____
$100,000		_____		_____		_____		_____
$200,000		_____		_____		_____		_____
$300,000		_____		_____		_____		_____

The first year after I began delegating unproductive tasks, my income rose from $15 per hour to over $50 per hour. In 1984, I earned in excess of $250 per hour. In 1985 it was over $300 per hour. Now I work less than six months of the year and earn in excess of $500 per hour. Every year I've surpassed the goal I set for myself, by fine tuning the management of my time. Today, I delegate absolutely everything which is unproductive that I can legally delegate.

IMPROVE YOUR "QUALITY OF LIFE"

Good Time Management techniques do not have to be used solely to increase one's income. They can be used to improve your "quality of life". Let's suppose you're happy with your current income. Your goal, as mine is, might be to spend the rest of your time at leisure activities with your family. Using your working time more "Efficiently" and "Effectively" will give you even more time to spend with your family. At the same time it will be easier to maintain your income level. As stated at the beginning of this Chapter, **"Time Management is both the Efficient and Effective use of one's time to achieve a goal"**.

" C H A P T E R 13 "

THE INITIAL
CLIENT INTERVIEW

In the past, instead of working according to a system,

I simply reacted to phone calls. I'd run off to meet prospects in front of a property, in a restaurant, or in a parking lot, because they said they wanted to see a property, immediately. I wouldn't do that today for the world!

The only way I'll show a property now, is if the prospect comes to my office for an initial interview, at a time we mutually agree on. This is usually within a week of when he calls. About once every 7 to 10 days I set aside a day or part of a day when I do nothing but initial client interviews.

The only exception I make to having a prospect come to my office for an initial client interview is when the prospect has an existing property he's going to sell. Then I go to their home to do a listing presentation. In all other cases they meet me in my office for the initial interview.

The interview procedure normally takes between an hour and a half and two hours. We discuss the clients' potential purchase in detail. And they engage me as their Personal Realtor, just as they'd engage a Lawyer or any other professional.

PURPOSES OF INITIAL CLIENT INTERVIEW

There are five main purposes for doing an initial client interview. I haven't listed them in any particular order as each one is as important as the other. They are as follows:

1. To get a pledge of loyalty;

2. To qualify the client financially;

3. To gain knowledge of the wants, needs and lifestyle of the client;

4. To alleviate doubts and concerns about purchasing or dealing with Realtors;

5. To sell yourself.

THE CLIENT INTERVIEW
STEP BY STEP

During the past few years, I've had literally hundreds of requests from readers wanting more detail about what should be covered during the Initial Client Interview. Below is a step by step outline of the points I cover. Since trade practices vary from one area to another it may be necessary to modify the content somewhat, but that should be easy to do.

1. RECORD PERSONAL DATA.
The first thing to do is record the names, addresses and phone numbers correctly. Get every possible phone number and address where the client might be reached, should you have to contact them for any reason, at any time in the future.

2. DISCUSS FINANCES

Next, get right to their finances. People generally feel uneasy discussing their finances with some one else, particularly someone they don't know. So get that out of the way right at the beginning. That way the balance of the interview is much more comfortable for everyone. Find out everything there is to know about their incomes. It's important to know if they're employed by someone else; if they're self-employed; whether they're remunerated by way of salary, commission, bonus or a combination thereof; if they receive any perks that could count as additional income when it's time to qualify for mortgaging, such as company cars, gas allowances, savings plans where contributions are matched by their employer etc.; if they have any additional sources of income such as interest from investments, rental income from other real estate they own and so on. Find out too, about all their debts and payment obligations.

Of course you want to know how much down payment they have and where it's coming from. Ask them if they had a larger down payment would they purchase a more expensive home than they're planning to purchase. If the answer is yes, and it usually is, discuss whether they have any sources from which they could obtain a larger down payment at little or no additional cost to them. The cash value of a life insurance policy they purchased years ago, mutual funds and pension funds are sources from which clients can sometimes obtain additional funds to increase their down payment.

I've had people come to see me about purchasing a home thinking they had only $10,000 or $15,000 down. When I examined their Life Insurance policy I found they had another $15,000 available at extremely low rates as a policy loan. They didn't realize they had the extra money available from a source where they couldn't be declined for the loan. They ended up buying a home for a substantially higher price with a bigger down payment. The same thing has happened with mutual fund plans and pension funds, particularly self administered pension plans belonging to close friends.

Explain that all this information is extremely important. Lenders will look at their debt service capabilities when determining if they qualify for a mortgage. Point out that you know the basic requirements of lenders in your area. Explain that sometimes by consolidating several debts into one, monthly payments and even interest rates can be lowered. Clients can then afford a higher mortgage payment than they thought they could. Explain that when you know their financial situation you won't waste their time and YOURS, inspecting properties they don't qualify for in terms of price and mortgaging.

3. PRICE RANGE — COMFORT ZONE

Discussing their finances leads directly to a determination of what price range they qualify for and what price range and monthly payment range they'll be comfortable with. Not everyone wants or needs a $250,000.00 home even though they may well qualify for one. Some people want to spend as much monthly as they qualify for. Others want a little breathing room left in the budget. What we want to determine here is what their "comfort zone" is.

4. MAP — AFFORDABLE AREAS

After discussing heavy and difficult personal finances with them, it's time to take a "sedative" — get relaxed — and become at ease with each other. At this point I take out a city map. Maps are great attention getters. People love looking at maps and trying to figure out where they are. It relaxes them. In fact, I've found that the map not only serves as a sedative but also as a "bonding agent", with most people during the Initial Client Interview.

Discuss the areas with housing in their price range. Talk about the amenities available in each area such as shopping centres, parks, arenas, swimming pools, libraries, schools, churches, synagogues, temples, mosques etc.. Point out the distances from their places of employment to different neighborhoods, the university, city centre etc.. Discuss the transportation alternatives that are available to get to schools, work, shopping, recreation and extracurricular activities. Zero in, as much as possible, on the kind of neighborhood they'd like to live in. Eliminate areas that are unsuitable for one reason or another. Target the areas they'll likely find suitable and should consider.

5. DESCRIBE YOUR PRESENT HOME

It's now time for them to describe their present home to you. Get them to describe their present home in detail. You want to know the style of home; the size; the colors of the exterior; the kind and color of the roof; the siding and the material; if there are decks or balconies; the size of the lot; the surrounding terrain and how it's landscaped. Get a description of the total interior room by room. Get room sizes, the decor, the materials used and what each of them consider the best features of their present home and why. Also get them to tell you what they dislike about the home and why.

Take extensive notes when they describe their present home. You want the clearest possible picture of their lifestyle that you can get. Then, you won't waste YOUR time and theirs looking at unsuitable homes. And they can purchase in the shortest time possible after you start looking.

If they're from out of town and you get to speak with them in advance, ask them to bring photos with them when they come, of the interior and exterior of their present home. I always insist on this with my out of town clients. It helps considerably. If you do this, not only do you get to see what their home looks like but you also get to see some of their furniture in the photos.

If they're local people, and rent, or own a home presently but won't be selling it when they purchase, you can have a look at where they presently live when you pick them up to go looking at homes the first time. This enables you to compare the description they gave you to their real life situation. It helps you envision how they see things.

6. MAKE A "WISH LIST"

During the previous exercise you did the writing. You made extensive notes about their present home as they described it to you. Now it's their turn. Get them to write out separate "wish lists" — things they'd like their new home to have. Have each of them do a separate list. Then get them to narrow the lists down to three or four items they consider most important. Explain you'll try to make appointments to inspect only homes that have these features. However point out you will not climinate homes that lack some of their preferences but have other interesting features they may not be aware of or haven't considered.

I always explain that in the Real Estate business we often hear the expression — "All Buyers Are Liars" — which has developed because people often buy a property which is the exact opposite to what they told their Realtor originally. So tell them not to be surprised if this happens to them to some degree — that they may settle for something with fewer or different features than they now anticipate.

Many items on clients "wish lists" have to be eliminated simply because of the differences in construction materials used, climate, planning regulations and varying economic conditions between one jurisdiction and another. When people move from southern to northern climates they may expect to purchase a home with a swimming pool only to find these do not exist. People who transfer to our area from Eastern Canada, for example, find to their dismay that it's next to impossible to purchase a brick home in many parts of Western Canada. In other cases the "wish list" has to be modified significantly because of difference in housing values between one region and another.

7. DISCUSS "HORROR STORIES"

We've all heard "horror stories" about people looking at 40 and 50 homes before finding the right one. Point out there's no need for that kind of thing to happen — not to them — or to anyone else. It only happens because people don't prepare properly for purchasing a home. Explain you're going through this process for the purpose of establishing guidelines and setting some definitive parameters. Get them to make a definite commitment to which basic floor plan they prefer.

Point out that if they prefer bungalows you won't be showing them anything else — you won't be showing them two-storeys if they'll only live in a bungalow. Tell them what you want to do is make this an easy enjoyable experience for them. Your aim: to find them a home the first day out and at the very most the second day. Hopefully, the first day you'll have chosen four or five homes, each of which will be so perfect for them, they'll have difficulty choosing which one they want. That's why you're having this interview — so you can do a real super job for them.

8. REVIEW THE OFFER TO PURCHASE FORM

Next, go through the offer form with them. Let them see it. Let them hold it in their hands. During the interview I go through it with clients clause by clause from beginning to end. I want them to become familiar with it — to feel comfortable and at ease with what is often a scary, mysterious document, especially to the novice purchaser. When it comes time to write an offer on a home they won't be intimidated by it if they familiarize themselves with it now. Discuss how one makes an offer, where the address of the property goes on the form, where the price is entered, where the deposit will be entered, how much it will have to be and when it has to be paid. Discuss whether they have the deposit readily available. If not, discuss how they can make interim arrangements so they can go ahead and make their purchase when they find the right home.

Discuss how and when the balance of the down payment has to be paid; where it is entered on the form; whether or not interim financing will be needed and how it can be arranged. Discuss where the amount being mortgaged gets entered on the form; how you'll make the offer "subject to" them obtaining a mortgage so they're protected and will get their deposit back, if for any reason a mortgage is unavailable to them. Show them where and how they can add additional terms and conditions to the offer to cover other concerns they might have.

Show them where the irrevocable date and the closing/possession dates are inserted. Discuss the significance of these. Go over all the standard clauses of your company offer form. Discuss what each means. Show them where they'll have to sign when they make an offer. Explain how counter offers/sign-backs work; how ultimately a meeting of the minds will be reached between them and the vendor/seller. When you're finished, they're no longer mystified as to what an offer is all about. They'll feel comfortable about signing and negotiating an offer when the time comes.

9. DISCLOSE ALL COSTS

Now it's time to discuss all the costs they'll incur when purchasing their home. Purchasers are often shocked when their lawyer/attorney informs them they need several hundred, and often several thousand dollars more, than they had budgeted for on closing. Transactions often collapse at this stage. The purchaser can't come up with the extra money. This happens because these items aren't discussed with clients when they should be. There is nothing more unprofessional on the part of a Realtor, than to fail to inform a client of ALL the costs and adjustments associated with closing a purchase. Yet, this is one of the more frequent public complaints against Realtors.

Make them aware they'll have legal fees to pay for both the transfer of title and placing of the mortgage. They'll have to pay for disbursements associated with the registration of the deed and mortgage documents. They'll have to reimburse their lawyer/attorney for other out of pocket expenses incurred on their behalf, such as courier charges, photocopies, long distance phone calls etc.. There'll be adjustments for such things as taxes, and in some jurisdictions for utilities and insurance. They may have to pay a "Land Transfer Tax" which **in some areas** amounts to hundreds and even thousands of dollars.

They might have such things as appraisal fees, application fees, administration fees and a surplus for the property tax account deducted from the mortgage proceeds depending on the lender they deal with. The mortgage company may require them to pay for a new survey of the property.

There may be fees associated with obtaining zoning confirmations and certificates of compliance from the city or municipal government. There may be escrow costs and interest adjustments and points to pay depending on the trade practices common to the area you live in.

These costs will vary greatly from one region to another. The point is that purchasers have a right to be fully informed about them and should be. Often, it's impossible to determine in advance, exactly what these costs will be. Always estimate on the high side. That way you can be sure you won't have unhappy purchasers.

10. MORTGAGE BROKER VERSUS OWN BANKER

I discuss why they should use a Mortgage Broker as opposed to simply using their own bank. (See Chapter 18 for a detailed discussion on this issue.)

11. A PROFESSIONAL INSPECTION

Discuss the wisdom of making their offer **"conditional on"** or **"subject to"** having the home inspected by a professional home inspection company. Recommend they pay the small fee (usually $250 - $350) to have the peace of mind of knowing the home is structurally sound; that the mechanical and electrical components are in good repair and satisfactory working order. The inspector will let them know what items may need replacing in the long and short term. I make them aware that when it comes to construction I know virtually nothing. I point out I'm not alone in this regard — that most Realtors are like me. I tell them that as we look at homes if they ask me, "What do you think of the furnace?", my answer will be, "It sure looks like one to me." I impress upon them that the only way to be sure is to have an inspection done by someone who is reputable and knows about these things. There are several reputable firms in our area who do these inspections and I'll be happy to recommend one.

Tell them the last thing you want is for them to buy something with problems. You'd rather sell them something else. Why? Because you're only interested in a long term Client/Realtor relationship. You want them to call you for all their future Real Estate needs. You want them to recommend you to their friends knowing you won't try to sell them anything with problems. Point out that when the time comes for them to sell in the future, the inspection company report will assist in marketing the home to someone else. If there's any one thing that builds confidence during an interview, it's the suggestion to have a professional home inspection done. This, together with the admission that you're not an expert on construction and mechanical matters, will alleviate any concerns they may have, that you're about to push them into a property that isn't right for them.

For the past eight years I've recommended the home inspection idea to all my clients. The majority of them take my advice. In that period of time I've only had two transactions where the inspector recommended the client not proceed with the purchase. In both cases there were serious, though not obvious, structural problems with the home in question. I sold both clients other properties without problems. I can't even begin to count the clients who've been referred to me because their friends have told them I recommended this procedure when they dealt with me. It is without doubt, the greatest confidence building practice I've ever adopted. And I strongly recommend this procedure to all Realtors.

12. THEY WON'T MISS ANYTHING

People often assume that by dealing exclusively with one Realtor they may be limiting their options to purchase certain properties. I assure them that by dealing with me nothing will be missed. I have a computer in both my office and my car. This provides instantaneous computerized access to the local MLS System 24 hours a day. I can show them anything that's listed on MLS in our area. And we can check at any time through the day to see if new listings have been added.

In the past 10 years I've never been refused cooperation by another Realtor on an exclusive listing. I point this out to them. I tell them that if I were refused cooperation on a property they were interested in, I'd be happy to go with them on their inspection. Together, we'd review all the listings and sales of similar properties in the area and make sure the property was a good deal. If they decided to go ahead with the purchase I'd be happy to represent them even if I wasn't getting paid, because they'd remember what I did for them and would make it up by referring others to me.

13. THOSE EMBARRASSING FSBO'S

"For Sale By Owner" properties are a fact of life. They're out there for all to see. So, we may as well deal with them right up front in the interview. I discuss the fact they may see a "For Sale By Owner" that appeals to them. I tell them that if they do they need not feel embarrassed. Instead, they should get hold of me right away. We'll handle things the same way I explained I'd handle an "Exclusive Listing" of another Realtor that I couldn't obtain cooperation from. I point out that the important thing is — **they get the right home.**

In ten years I've only had one client who purchased a "For Sale By Owner". He did it on his own without me being aware of it. He called me after the transaction closed. He said he was too embarrassed to call me before. By this time he was having second thoughts about the wisdom of his new investment. He wanted me to tell him if he got a good buy. He had purchased privately from a lawyer. He paid cash down to an existing first mortgage. Before I arrived at his home I was hoping for the best. But that wasn't the case. He paid at least $15,000.00 more than the property was worth. This happens frequently with "For Sale By Owner" transactions.

Up to that time I'd never covered the **"For Sale By Owner"** issue in my interviews. Now, because of what happened to Paul, I tell his story in every interview. And he has told me time and again, to tell my clients to call him if they have any doubts about how easily the same thing could happen to them. Dealing with the "Exclusive Listing" and the "For Sale By Owner" issues in this manner during the interview, builds confidence. It also assures the client you're not going to push them into something just for the sake of earning a commission.

14. "THRESHOLD RIGHTS"

In many areas the local Real Estate Boards have established what are referred to as "Threshold Rights". Simply put, this means that if a Realtor shows a client a property, that Realtor is entitled to the commission on any sale of that property to that client, even if the client purchases that property through another Realtor at a later date. If these rights apply in your area they need to be covered in your interview.

"Threshold Rights" can create difficult situations when clients are out open-housing and see a property they're interested in. You have to tell your clients that if they don't handle the situation properly you could end up not getting paid even if you sell them the home. Make sure they understand that if they go through an open-house on their own, they shouldn't give their names out under any circumstances. Tell them to tell the host or hostess they have their own Realtor, with whom they will be dealing exclusively, and to ask if under those circumstances, they can take a walk through. Tell them to go ahead if the answer is "yes". If it's "no" tell them to leave, call you, and you'll make an appointment to take them through later.

Tell them not to fall for the usual sales pitches such as, "I'm presenting an offer on it right after the Open House. If you want a chance to buy it you'll have to let me write it up right now" or, "It's an exclusive and I'm not cooperating with any other Realtors. If you want it you'll have to deal with me anyway" or, any other sales pitch aimed at getting them to deal with the Realtor sitting the Open House rather than you.

Also, tell them it's better if they don't call on newspaper ads, but rather let you check out any ads they're interested in. However, tell them if they do call on newspaper ads not to leave their name or phone number. Just get the information and say they have their own Realtor.

15. GET PLEDGE OF LOYALTY

At the end of the interview obtain a pledge of loyalty from them. And that's exactly what to do!! Don't assume they're going to be loyal because you got along well, or because they were nice people or whatever. **This is serious business!** It's going to involve YOUR time and expertise. You don't want an implied agreement. You want nothing short of a firm commitment.

Here's how I get it. I say, "Now before we go looking at houses or do anything else I need your loyalty. I need to know that you're not going to deal with anyone but me. That's the only way I or any Realtor can do a proper job for you. If you deal with me today, another Realtor tomorrow and someone else the following day, everyone of us will feel we have to push you into something when we're with you. After all, tomorrow you'll be out looking with someone else. We may never see you again. I'm not interested in that kind of relationship. Under those conditions, I can't do a good job for you. I want you to hire me as your EXCLUSIVE PERSONAL REALTOR. You do that, and I'm prepared to work as hard as necessary to ensure you get what's right for you. ARE YOU PREPARED NOW — TO GIVE ME YOUR LOYALTY?" I then shut up. I look them straight in the eye. I don't say another word until they give me their answer. If the answer is "no" — and that doesn't happen very often — we terminate the interview and I don't have any further involvement with them.

Since the answer is usually "yes", we determine how we'll go about things. We make a future appointment to begin looking. My goal: sell them the first day out, after looking at three to five homes.

16. IT WON'T TAKE LONG TO BUY
The last thing to do before they leave is to point out that it won't take long to buy. I tell them not to be at all surprised if they buy the first day out and that most of the people I deal with do.

VERY EFFECTIVE TIME
MANAGEMENT TOOL

The "Initial Client Interview" is a very effective "Time Management" tool. Most of the people I deal with purchase the first day out. And rarely does it go beyond the second day. I'd never be able to do this without first having done an interview to qualify them properly.

When a new prospect calls I explain my procedure. If they won't come for an interview and insist on meeting me in front of a property right away, I politely tell them this is not the way I work. I offer to have another Realtor show them the property.

If they accept my offer I refer them to another Realtor on the understanding that if a sale is made to them by that Realtor I get a 25% referral fee. The result is that I don't get stood up miles from anywhere. Nor do I waste gas and valuable time. These should be spent on better quality prospects.

Occasionally someone fails to show up for an interview appointment. When this happens I just slot in another client or another job that's been waiting.

PEOPLE HAPPY TO
WAIT FOR INTERVIEW

Most people are happy to wait a few days and come for an interview after I explain why I follow this procedure.

I explain that I have all the latest information on properties in every area of the city available through my computer at my office.

I also point out that I have information on all the amenities available in each area. When we meet we can determine where all public, separate, ethnic, specialized and private schools, colleges and the university are located.

After we meet they'll know about all the recreational facilities, lakes and parks with various types of programs and their locations. They will be familiar with the locations of churches and other places of worship in each area.

I can provide them with computer print-outs on various areas. These will show how much various properties are listed for. They'll also show what properties in various areas have sold for recently. They can become "market wise" very quickly by coming for an interview.

I explain we can cut several days off the home hunting routine by proceeding in this manner. I also tell them, if for any reason either they or I do not feel comfortable with each other after the interview, we do not have to do business with each other.

The initial interview saves the client much unnecessary running around and saves the Realtor many valuable hours.

That makes us both winners!

THE RATING SYSTEM
FOR SHOWING PROPERTY

As mentioned in the previous chapter my objective

when showing property is to sell the client the first day out and at most on the second day. The client interview allows me to take charge of the home finding mission on behalf of the client. It gives me an insight into the likes and dislikes of the client. It provides a basis on which to make some exciting choices to show them.

PLAY THE RATE
AND NAME GAME

I start the mission off by telling the client we're going to make their home buying fun. I get my clients to do two things when we're looking at homes. The first is I get them to play the **"name game"**. We give each house a silly or distinctive name. The reason? In addition to adding an element of fun, at the end of our tour we'll have no trouble remembering which house we're referring to.

It's far easier and far less confusing to remember what a house is like, if you refer to it by a silly or distinctive name, than it is to remember it by address. After a viewing we don't leave the driveway until they name the house. If they really like a particular home, or some specific feature about it, I'll help by suggesting they use their own descriptive adjectives to name it. If for example they say, "What a perfect view!!", when they see a certain house, then I'll suggest we name that one "PERFECT VIEW".

The second thing I get them to do is rate the homes as we view them. They rate them according to choice; IE first, second and third choice. They rate each one after we view it. In addition to rating the homes we see, they have to keep a **"consideration list"**. However, they're only allowed to keep their three top choices on the "consideration list". No more. That means when we've looked at the fourth house, they have to decide which three are to remain on the list.

This process serves three purposes. Firstly, it keeps them focussed on their three top choices at all times throughout the tour. That after all is what they have to do if we're going to conclude a purchase quickly. Secondly, it gets them making definite decisions. That too is what they have to do if we're going to conclude a purchase quickly. Thirdly, it gives me some clear insight into what they really want. And that's also important if we're going to conclude a transaction quickly.

Once a property is bumped from the list it doesn't get discussed again. After looking at the first four we don't look at the next choice until we've eliminated one of the previous choices. As stated earlier, at all times throughout the tour I want the clients to focus their attention on their three top choices only.

TIME FOR A
<u>SECOND LOOK</u>

At the end of the tour I always suggest we go back and have a second look at their first choice. It usually looks better the second time and we discuss making an offer. If they hesitate I tell them to think about it. But I get them to make me two promises. The first is that they'll make a firm decision — either make an offer or put the property out of their mind completely. The second promise is that they'll let me know by a predetermined time so we know whether to arrange additional showings the following day.

Many times clients will decide to offer on their first choice before we even complete our initial tour. And often they decide to write an offer on the spot after having the second look at their first choice at the conclusion of the tour. Sometimes they need a little more time to make a decision and will call back later having decided to make an offer.

In other cases another tour is required the following day or another day. I closely observe the process they use in eliminating properties, in order to focus on their three top choices only, during our initial tour. As a result it's exceptionally easy for me to zero in on what they want and like on our second day out. Rarely does it take more than a second tour of showings to sell a client a home.

When showing houses I keep a sheet on each property where we list the address and the name the clients have given the property. I write down both my comments and the clients comments regarding the property. I have my assistant pass on these comments to the listing Realtors. They always appreciate the feedback. In addition these comments are useful when I'm setting up showings for other clients.

Use the rating system outlined above when showing property to clients. You'll be amazed at how much more productive your selling time can be.

You'll also be amazed at how much happier your clients — and their Realtor too — will be.

" C H A P T E R 15 "

CERTIFYING
CHEQUES

Years ago I quit running all over town to certify

cheques. In fact, I don't even send my assistant to do that. It's such a time waster. I send a courier instead. Yet, I see Realtors drive right across the city, stand in line for 3/4 of an hour, and drive back after getting a cheque certified. They waste a whole morning doing a job a courier is happy to do for $10. I believe one's time is better spent on direct income generating activities.

One solution to this time wasting problem is to arrange for a courier service to come to your office each day at a certain time, and pick up all the cheques that need to be certified that day. Usually a reasonable fee can be worked out with the courier service — especially if it's to be an ongoing detail.

PUTTING
UP SIGNS

Hardly a day goes by that I don't see Realtors putting up signs. This is another time waster. Someone else can do it a lot cheaper. I hire a Sign Maintenance Company. When they're out putting up signs I'm making a listing presentation; showing a property; doing a client interview or presenting an offer.

REMEMBER THE
DELEGATION RULE

Couriers and Sign Companies don't cost $500 per hour. Nor can I earn $500 an hour putting up signs or standing in Bank lineups waiting to get deposit cheques certified.

Remember, if someone else can perform the task for less than you are worth per hour it should be delegated, unless there is a compelling reason why it shouldn't be. Exceptions to this rule should be few and far between.

" C H A P T E R 16 "

BEWARE NEGATIVE
NON ACHIEVERS

Going to the office wastes time. So, I rarely go there.

If you want to waste two hours — go to the office for five minutes. If you have to go to the office, go before anyone else gets there in the morning or after they've all gone at night.

That way you can avoid discussing the economy and all of it's pitfalls with the **"Resident Economists"**. Every office has these **Time Wasting Negative Doomsayers**. They come to the office daily with reams of bad news about interest rates, trade deficits, the weak dollar, and a thousand other explanations why the country is going down the tubes.

They tell you why the market is bad. According to them everyone who is doing well is being fed by the Manager. Or, they get all their business because of who their in-laws are. Or better still, their spouse knows somebody with good connections.

Besides the **"Resident Economists"** there are the **"Office Politicians"**. Every office has them too. They call you aside; they want your opinion on any number of things they think should be changed about how the office is run. They complain. They aren't doing well. According to them, it's all because of office policies.

If the office only had a more impressive board room and two more closing rooms, everyone would somehow do a lot better. That's this month's project. Every time you see them they have a new campaign on the go. What's worse? They want you to get involved! Tell them you're too busy to get involved, and they get upset because you won't support them in their only goal: Change For The Sake Of Change.

Beware also, the **"Social Gadfly Types"**. They spend their lives organizing socials — for themselves and others in the office. Every time you go in they take you aside. You soon realize they're more concerned with their social life, than with the fact they haven't had a sale in a month or more.

When you tell them you don't have time for a drink in the middle of the day because you're too busy, they accuse you of contributing to the lack of spirit in the office. The question is — Which Spirit? It never dawns on them, that you may have joined the company to make a living — not to broaden your social circle. In their eyes you're weird. You're a Realtor for a reason that makes no sense to them at all — you WORK!

I'm not talking about the person or persons responsible for organizing the annual Christmas Party or Golf Tournament or other annual company events. I'm referring to those types who would have you party every day — the chronic pool player; daily happy hour attender; etc.

Every office has its **"Professional Time Wasters"** — **the Resident Economists, Politicians and Social Gadflies**. They're all negative non-achievers. To avoid falling into the same rut, you have to put distance between these people and yourself. If you're going to be successful you can't afford to associate with negative people who waste your time.

My way of avoiding this pitfall is to stay away from the office, except on rare occasions when protocol requires my attendance. Since most trips to the office are for pick up or delivery of documents they're made by my assistant or driver.

NO REFLECTION
ON MANAGEMENT

At seminars I quite often deal with the subject of the office Time Wasters. Frequently, I'm approached afterwards by managers and owners who take a very defensive position vis-a-vis their office and this problem. They claim they don't have this type of person working in their office. Unfortunately, they interpret what was said as if it were intended to be a put-down of their management abilities.

I want to emphasize here that nothing in this Chapter is in any way intended to convey the impression that offices are poorly managed. Nor is it intended to reflect negatively on the ability of owners or managers to hire the right kind of employees. Quite the contrary. On reflection, I have to admit that every office I ever worked in was well managed. At the same time I know that some offices aren't.

I readily admit that in the past I wrongly blamed office policies for my failure to do better. I also admit that at one time I wasn't doing very well because I socialized too much. And yes, I even influenced other licensees to waste their time. And you know something else? It wasn't the fault of the manager! How could it be? He didn't know, and could not he be expected to know, what more than 40 salespeople were doing or saying at all times.

The point is simple. Human nature being what it is, there is no way to avoid having some Negative Time Waster Types in any office that employs more than a few people. That is a fact.

It's also a fact that in the Real Estate Profession you can't earn much money hanging around the office. And it's true, if salespeople do hang around the office they'll have no shortage of companionship.

It's also true that a third party can be a negative influence on one person and not on another. For example, there may be nothing inherently wrong with the well-heeled gentleman who is licensed with your office, doesn't work very hard and wants someone to spend the last seven hours of every day with him, at the pool hall up the street. To other salespeople, not as well off financially and needing to earn a living, that well-heeled fellow could become the catalyst for their failure — if they're not careful. Yet, to another financially independent licensee he might simply be great company.

The point is, that as salespeople, we have to decide for ourselves who makes a positive contribution to our success and distance ourselves sufficiently from those who do not. **Management can't do that for us!**

" C H A P T E R   17 "

WHEN A CONTRACT IS SIGNED
CALL UP THE RESERVES

If you want to sell any product to more people, you

have to spend more of your time, with people who are going to purchase your product. Let me repeat that with more emphasis! **IF YOU WANT TO SELL ANY PRODUCT TO MORE PEOPLE, YOU HAVE TO SPEND MORE OF YOUR TIME, WITH PEOPLE WHO ARE GOING TO PURCHASE YOUR PRODUCT.** If you sell a client today, and spend tomorrow tidying up loose ends, you're losing money.

Once A Deal Is Made, Begin Spending Your Time, With A New Prospect. In other words, get on to the next client immediately!! Have someone else tidy up the loose ends. **"When the contract is signed, call up the reserves."** That's my motto.

TWO TYPES OF CONTRACTS

In our business, there are two types of contracts that make us money: the Sales Contract and the Listing Contract. When I get a Sales Contract signed my assistants take over. They certify the cheque; put the sold stickers on; take the sign down on closing; fill in the Lawyer's names and other conveyancing information on the agreement; canvass the area; etc.

The same procedure applies when I get a Listing Contract signed. As soon as it's signed I hand it over to my aides. They confirm the measurements; put up the sign; get keys cut and delivered to other offices for convenient pickup; canvass the area; prepare and put information sheets in the home; put the lock-box on; fill out all necessary forms and turn them into the office.

When the RESERVES are doing this, my efforts go into listing or selling other properties, and the cycle continues.

" C H A P T E R   18 "

MORTGAGING — THE
TIME SAVING WAY!

In the last Chapter we talked about my motto: "**When**

the contract is signed, call up the reserves." In other words: **"Get out of the picture when your job is done."** A Realtor's job is done or should be done when an offer is accepted. This applies whether or not a mortgage needs to be arranged.

GET YOURSELF
A GOOD BROKER

If a mortgage needs to be arranged turn the client over to an expert — a Mortgage Broker or Mortgage Banker who is part of your team of reserves. If your team doesn't include a Mortgage expert get one lined up, immediately! Arrange to have him or her handle all your transactions — the easy ones and the tough ones — for a prearranged fee.

By giving all your transactions to a single broker, you'll be amazed at the deal you can make on brokerage fees. Depending on your volume, you can perhaps get a Broker to do your transactions for as little as $300 - $500 per deal.

WHY A
BROKER?

I recommend using a Broker as opposed to a Bank or Trust Company Mortgage Officer. Why? There are several reasons. We'll discuss the two most important here.

The first is OBJECTIVITY. I want whoever is doing mortgages for my clients to be Objective. A Bank or Trust Company Mortgage Officer can only offer what his own company has in the way of mortgage products. Furthermore, he can qualify clients based only on his own company guidelines.

A good Broker can offer clients a variety of products and options. He can place mortgages with any number of companies that have varying guidelines for qualification, fitting the particular needs and circumstances of almost any client. For example, my Broker is often able to place mortgages for my clients with the Alberta Treasury Branch. They have completely Open, Fixed Rate Mortgages at competitive rates.

I never discuss specific terms of mortgaging with my clients. So when this happens you can be sure the clients are happy they went to my Broker. They know when they go to sell later they won't have to pay a penalty to get out of their mortgage.

There are several other reasons I recommend a Broker. The most important one regards TURN DOWNS. If a client is turned down for some reason by one Lender, he still deals with the same person. In fact, if he's dealing with a Broker he usually won't even know he was turned down by a Lender. The Broker simply places the deal with someone else.

If a client is dealing with a Bank or Trust Company Loans Officer and gets turned down, he has to begin dealing all over again with someone new. This often leads to problems for the client. After being turned down once or twice, subsequent Loans Officers often treat the application from a position of suspicion.

Good Brokers are like good Realtors. They know their business. They know their Lenders. Just like a good Realtor knows how to present an offer in a way his client is most likely to accept it, a good Broker knows how to present a mortgage package to his Lender so that it will be accepted.

BROKER FEES — WHO PAYS?

Once you have established a fixed fee with a competent Broker it's easier to answer the question of who pays the Brokerage Fee. I apprise my clients of the reasons why they should deal with an independent objective expert when they arrange their mortgage. I tell them what his fee is. In most cases they do not object to paying a few hundred dollars for expert advice.

In the case of Company transfers there is very seldom a problem in this regard. The company usually picks up the bill.

If a client really objects, I first offer to split the fee. If that doesn't do the trick I pay it all. The fact is, that if I had to pay the full fee in every case, I would.

OBJECTIVE — DO INCOME GENERATING ACTIVITY

The objective is to keep yourself free of the time consuming duties of arranging mortgages. In many cases this takes longer than making a sale. While the Broker arranges the mortgage you can make another sale or write another listing. Your commission on another sale or listing will be far greater than the few hundred dollars you pay a Broker for putting the mortgage together on the first one.

In the last ten years I haven't had a single client refuse this service. After we discuss it thoroughly, and they understand the complexity of the mortgage business, they're happy to see an expert and pay what is basically a small fee.

LET THE BROKER DO THE LEG WORK

Choosing a Mortgage Broker is a lot like choosing a Lawyer, Doctor or any other Professional. Interview all the Mortgage Brokers in your area. Tell them if you select them, all your mortgage business will be directed their way. Make it clear that they'll have to do the legwork, which will include getting the condition removal or waiver forms signed and delivered to you, when the commitments are obtained.

While your broker is doing the legwork and arranging the mortgage, you can be selling or listing another property. This is clearly a case of making better use of your time. Remember, if the task you are about to perform, can be done by someone else for less than you are worth per hour, it should be delegated unless there is a compelling reason why it shouldn't be!

SOME DO'S AND
SOME DON'TS

Do tell your Broker if you favor a certain Lawyer/Attorney. He can make sure his Lenders have his name on their list of approved Lawyers/Attorneys. The Broker can have the Lawyer/Attorney act for the Lender on your deals. He can recommend the Lawyer/Attorney to the clients as well if they don't already have their own.

Don't give the Broker ridiculous deadlines to meet — such as five days to arrange a mortgage. Tell him that whenever possible you'll give him 21 days.

There is nothing more senseless than demanding a mortgage in five days, when a transaction doesn't close for two months or more. All that is accomplished by such inconsiderate action, is that everyone in the approval process gets upset. Your client may even find himself with a less favorable deal than he might otherwise have received.

In addition, short conditional periods for mortgaging make unnecessary paperwork for Realtors. For certain, extra forms will need to be signed extending the condition. When I receive an offer on one of my listings with a ridiculously short condition for financing, I advise my

Vendor to "Sign it Back" extending the time to a reasonable period. I'm too busy, and so are my Vendors, to be signing unnecessary forms only because an inconsiderate Realtor has no respect for other people's time.

DON'T LOSE
YOUR OBJECTIVITY

Aside from making better use of your time there is another equally valid reason for getting out of the picture at the right time.

Too often over the years I've seen clients, totally happy with their Realtor at the time an offer was accepted, become frustrated and downright unhappy, when the Realtor couldn't produce a mortgage at the bargain basement terms the clients were led to expect. I've seen the same thing happen over legal fees.

This kind of problem develops when Realtors lose their objectivity. They get emotionally involved with the client. Instead of getting out of the picture at the right time, Realtors attempt to obtain unreasonable bargains for clients.

In some cases it goes farther than others. I've seen Realtors become so protective of clients they'd accompany them to mortgage interviews. They end up being embarrassed when asked by the client to leave so they can talk confidentially to the Lender.

When clients realize the bargain the Realtor promised is not to be found, they become unhappy and upset.

Instead of sending friends to the Realtor, as they would have if he or she had gotten out of the picture when their job was done, they refer their friends to other Realtors.

There is no valid reason for a Realtor to attempt to secure bargains from other participants in a Real Estate transaction, on behalf of his clients. In fact, there is every reason not to. The result more often than not, will be unhappy clients.

When clients ask, I tell them I will recommend them to the best person in the business. Items such as Legal Fees and Mortgage Terms are dictated among other things, by circumstances peculiar to each individual. These items should be arranged privately between the parties involved.

GOING QUOTES AREN'T GOING RATES

I always quote mortgage rates at least 1% to 1 1/2% higher than **"Going Quotes"**. I've learned after 25 years in the business that what are passed off as **"Going Rates"** should be referred to as **"Going Quotes"**. When clients tell me they think there are better rates around, I simply point out that rates vary from company to company and from day to day. There's no magic involved. They'll have to pay the **"Going Rate"** at the time.

I tell them the best I can do is turn them over to an expert on completion of their purchase. That expert will help them arrange the best deal available. It will be based on their own peculiar financial circumstances. I explain that it's impossible for any Realtor, or any customer, to keep abreast of all the latest developments in the mortgage business.

I point out there are hundreds of Banks, Trust Companies, Credit Unions, Life Insurance Companies, Mortgage Companies, Savings and Loan Companies, Government Agencies, and other Lenders, all with ever changing policies out there in the marketplace.

I stress the interest rate is not the only important aspect of a Mortgage. Even if all companies charged exactly the same rate there would be vast differences in the privileges and terms offered by various companies. For example, the way companies set their interest rate is more important than what the rate is on any given day. What counts is, what the rate will be the day the clients get the money. Today, there are as many ways of setting the interest rate as there are Lenders.

As a result it's conceivable that the company quoting the lowest rate today could be the company with the highest rate the day money is advanced. A good objective independent Broker can safeguard your clients from pitfalls like this.

For these and many other reasons, anyone purchasing real estate should see an expert. Experts deal with a variety of companies. They can offer advice on all the pros and cons of mortgaging. I also tell clients that if they have a preference when it comes to Lenders, my expert can do the mortgage with that Lender. He'll do all the legwork for them. This will save them having to take time off work to make applications, etc., and is usually much appreciated.

PENALTIES FOR
EARLY PAY-OUT

Good advice from an objective Broker will save a purchaser his fee many times over. The average person should steer clear of something as complex as arranging their own mortgage. It's usually the largest amount of money they'll ever borrow. For a decision of that magnitude everyone should have the best advice available.

Among other things, a good Broker can place your clients Mortgages with Lenders who are easy to negotiate pay-outs with. Remember, they're likely to be reselling the property in 2 1/2 to 3 years. They, as well as you, want all the flexibility they can have at that time.

Some Lenders spell out early repayment penalties clearly in their mortgage documents. Many do not. When these obligations are not spelled out in black and white, the cost of early repayment can be exorbitant. Most Realtors have had a case where a Lender has refused to allow early repayment at all.

We do no favours to ourselves or anyone else, by allowing clients who qualify for better terms to obtain mortgages from these kinds of Lenders. When clients are faced with huge prepayment penalties, the quarter percent lower rate they may have gotten when they acquired the mortgage often pales by comparison.

" C H A P T E R   19 "

LISTINGS AND
TIME MANAGEMENT

The consistent Top Producers in the Real Estate

Profession — those who lead in commissions earned in good and bad times alike — generally have one thing in common. They're all "**Good Listers**".

FORGET SELLING — BECOME A GOOD LISTER!

New licensees approach me all the time. They want to get started on the right foot. I always tell them, "**Forget about trying to sell Real Estate. Concentrate on learning to become a Good Lister. When you become a Good Lister the Sales will take care of themselves.**"

I offer the same advice to veteran Realtors, too. Often they approach me looking for advice on how to "**Get Out Of A Slump.**" Without exception, when they take my advice it's not long before it's business as usual again. And they learn, that if they're going to continue to succeed in this business, they simply have to become "**Good Listers**".

GOOD LISTERS NEVER FIND THEMSELVES IN A "SLUMP"!! They don't know what the word means. They're "**SLUMP PROOF**". You can be too. All you have to do is LEARN how to become a "**Good Lister**". I learned a long time ago, that having more listings is the "cure", for virtually all of the problems the Real Estate Market can place in the way of a Realtor.

I hasten, however, to advise all who come to see me, and all who read this book, that becoming a "**Good Lister**" doesn't happen without a great deal of effort, study and practice. The effort and practice you can provide yourself. But what about material one can study to learn the basics of becoming a **"Good Lister"**?

In our Profession we're fortunate. We can purchase a book that without question is the best "How To" book available to practitioners of any profession. I refer to **"Real Estate Listing Magic", a book by California Realtor Gael Himmah**.

In 1990 Mr. Himmah published the "Master Addition" of this book. It's available from Gael Himmah Publishing Company, P.O. Box 4591, Walnut Creek, Calif. 94596.

It's one book that should be in every Realtor's library. If I had known about it when I first started in Real Estate, I'd have tasted success much sooner than I did. The first step to becoming a "Good Lister" is to get yourself a copy. Follow the procedures outlined by Mr. Himmah religiously.

Obviously if a subject is so broad that a book can be written about it, then it's impossible to deal with the topic in all aspects in a single chapter. For this reason we're only going to discuss a limited number of points here. These are generally relevant to Good Effective Time Management, and especially significant in making a Listing presentation.

MOST COMMON
VENDOR/SELLER COMPLAINT

The most common complaint Vendors/Sellers make about Realtors is, that once a property has been listed, the

Realtor pulls a disappearing act. If they hear from the Realtor at all, it isn't until the Listing expires. They get a call then asking them to re-list.

How is a Vendor/Seller supposed to feel if he is treated in this manner?

In many cases, Realtors do a good job of promoting a Listing behind the scenes. However, for some reason they don't communicate their efforts to the Vendor/Seller. He is left with the impression the Realtor did little or nothing to sell his property.

To say the least, it's a sad commentary on our profession.

TWO EASY SOLUTIONS

There are two easy solutions to this communications problem.

The first involves calling the Vendor/Seller every week and updating him on your progress. Using this method takes time. You do all the work. If you use this method though, you'll have no trouble re-listing when the expiration date comes round.

The second method I like better. With it the Vendor/Seller does the work. It's the method I use. It really works wonders! When I list a property I tell my Vendor/Seller that I can't do it all by myself. I need his help. He needs mine. We're in this thing together!

TRAIN YOUR VENDOR/SELLER
TO CALL YOU

Communication is important. The Vendor/Seller expects me to do a proper job of selling his home. He . . . . Has To Keep Me Informed!

I list nearly everything on MLS. On our MLS system we make our appointments directly with the owner unless the Listing instructs otherwise. I explain to my Vendor/Seller, that I expect a phone call from him, every time the property is shown.

I want him to call and give me the name and phone number, of every Realtor, who shows his property. Only if he does this, can I conduct a proper follow-up with the Realtor.

I tell him to leave the information with whoever answers the phone at my office. I explain there's no need to talk to me directly. All we need is the information. Other Realtors often convince their clients to offer on my listing instead of another, when we follow up on showings.

SELL YOUR LISTINGS
TO OTHER REALTORS

Not long after I first obtained my licence an old Realtor gave me some sage advice. I've never forgotten it. He said, **"Most of the sales you make in this business won't earn you a nickel's worth of income. You won't get** paid for them at all. Yet, if you don't make these free sales you won't be in the business long. These sales aren't made to the general public. They're the ones you make over and over again, day in and day out, to other Realtors. You see, in this business you literally have to sell every listing to an endless number of Realtors, before you get an acceptable offer from one of THEIR clients."

Was my old friend right? You bet he was! It pays to follow up with Realtors who show your listings. It's an ideal time to sell the property they showed plus your other listings to them.

A VENDOR/SELLER'S MORTAL SIN

On my list of Vendors/Sellers I check off those who call me each week. If they haven't called by the end of two weeks it means one of two things. Either they haven't been getting showings, or they're guilty of not communicating with their Realtor. In my book that's a Mortal Sin!

In the latter case, I remind them of their responsibility in our partnership — that of getting their home sold. From then on we usually get a call every time there is a showing.

WHAT! NO CALLS?
IS THE PRICE TOO HIGH?

If there are no calls — and no showings — it's time for some serious talk. We discuss why that might be. Perhaps other Realtors think the price is too high.

There isn't a more effective method of keeping communications alive that I know of. The onus is placed on the Vendor/Seller. He soon realizes there is something wrong if he isn't getting showings. He often concludes on his own that it may be the price.

Even though the Vendor/Seller does the calling when you use this method, he'll never say he didn't hear from you after you listed the property. He feels proper attention has been paid to him. Yet, all you did was get him involved.

I carry over 50 listings most of the time. Seldom do I have to call more than one or two of my Vendors/Sellers in any given week.

SECOND MOST COMMON
VENDOR/SELLER COMPLAINT

The second most common complaint Vendors/Sellers have about Realtors, is that they make all kinds of promises to get a listing and then fail to keep any of them. Unlimited newspaper advertising was promised and didn't materialize. Public open houses every weekend were promised and didn't materialize. A sale within thirty days was promised and guess what? It didn't materialize either!

Get the picture?

When I find myself competing with other Realtors for a listing I usually win. Here's why. At the beginning of the book I told you about the profound statement that changed my life as a Realtor. **"If you want to be AVERAGE do what everyone else in your business does. If you want to be ABOVE AVERAGE do the opposite."** You know, that really works!

In virtually every competition for a Listing, I know what my competition is going to tell the property owner. They'll promise plenty of Advertising, more Public Open Houses and if I'm lucky, maybe even a Quick Sale! If there are two competitors, the owner will hear the same story twice. If there are three, he'll hear it three times. When it's all over, I'm the only one with an opposite approach.

DON'T MAKE
PROMISES

I inform every Vendor/Seller I deal with I don't Newspaper Advertise property. I tell him I don't hold Public Open Houses. I make him aware that statistics dictate that it takes 80 — 120 days to sell a properly priced average home in our present market. He's usually shocked. He hasn't heard this before! Of course, I provide some other facts and information that no one else bothers to provide either. Because my presentation is different I make an impression.

I tell him that based on our statistics, only one in every 360-400 people ever buy the property they call on. I emphasize most people buy a home approximately $15,000 more expensive than the one they call on. The reason for that is that most people shop for bargains. Like he does. He relates to that.

His home then, will most likely sell to someone who calls on a home priced about $15,000 lower than his. And, if I advertise his home I'm likely going to sell any prospect who calls me on the ad a home belonging to someone else which will sell for about $15,000 more than his. Why then, should he be concerned about his home being advertised in the newspaper?

I explain that Realtors advertise properties to get clients, not to sell specific homes. Real Estate offices therefore, advertise homes with features that make people call. If his home doesn't have those features it likely wouldn't get advertised anyway.

As for Open Houses I make them aware Realtors sit these to get clients. Now and then, on the odd and rare occasion, the house they are sitting sells to someone who comes through an Open House. I explain that it's like having a lottery to get a buyer for his home. The odds are about the same. I prefer to get clients using other methods. I am always booked two to three weeks in advance with referrals and repeat clients. I show them my diary. I always have appointments booked with several transfers from other cities. Any one of them may be interested in his home.

These are qualified purchasers. Many of them "Need to Buy" to take advantage of company benefits. They are not unknown quantities who walk in off the street. They are not people about whom we know nothing. I point out

I will not be kicking them out of their home so I can get clients for myself — clients who are likely to buy someone else's home rather than theirs.

I have other Realtors call me regularly. They want to sit Open Houses on my listings. Often they end up selling one of my listings, where they sat an Open House, to a client they get from another source. This happens because they get to know and like the listing. I explain this to my Vendors/Sellers. For that reason they'll occasionally let another Realtor sit a Public Open House. In this case the objective is not to sell it to someone who comes through, but rather to get another Realtor turned on about the property.

LIST FOR LONG TERM
AND CANCEL ANYTIME

I don't usually write listings for less than four months. I often take them for six months to a year depending on the marketability of the property. I tell my Vendors/Sellers I'll cancel the listing, anytime they're not happy with my services. I offer to give them a letter to this effect, signed by my agent and myself. In the past seven years, I've cancelled no more than ten listings. Several of them I got back later.

I don't need unhappy clients running around the country "Bad Mouthing" me. Studies indicate that for every unhappy client, an additional 140 people don't deal with you. I'd rather have them tell their friends I didn't force an incompatible relationship on them, than tell them what a rotten Realtor I happen to be.

In the few cases where I've ended up cancelling a listing it was usually the result of a personality problem.

In most cases I was the one who instigated the termination. We've all met the odd impossible Vendor/Seller. When I see a problem developing I would rather cancel the listing.

If I sense a problem when I go to write a listing, I pass. I'm always wary of the Vendor/Seller who was unhappy with someone I know to be a good Realtor. If a Vendor/Seller is running down another good Realtor and you take his listing, chances are you'll be his next victim. I usually tell these types I don't have the time to give them the attention they need.

The fact of the matter is, that if cancellation privileges are offered very few Vendors/Sellers take you up on them. It's better to lose the odd one that way and get your listings written for a longer term, than it is to be rewriting listings that expire every month or two. In fact, I adjust the term I write my listings for if the market is such that a longer average time is required to sell the property.

Since implementing my "Cancel Anytime Policy" I no longer have to sell hard to get listings for a longer term. In fact, Vendors/Sellers usually don't care how long I take the listing for.

I try to make sure that I write my listings for at least a month longer than the average time it takes to sell a listing. At present in Calgary that tends to be between 80-120 days if priced properly. So I presently write my listings for a minimum five month term.

CONCENTRATE ON PRICING RIGHT

In addition to cutting down tremendously on the paper work required to frequently re-list property, it puts the law of averages on my side. Instead of spending a lot of time selling the Vendor/Seller on a longer expiration date, I deal with getting the listing priced right.

If, after reviewing a proper analysis of current market conditions the owner insists on trying to get a higher price I still take the listing. I try to get him to agree to a reduction policy. Within three weeks, if there isn't sufficient action we'll reduce to the price indicated by the market analysis. I also try to get Vendors/Sellers to agree to a price reduction every 30 days if warranted by market conditions.

OVER PRICED LISTINGS EARN BIG COMMISSIONS

Even if a Vendor/Seller will not list at what I consider to be a proper price, I will take his listing anyway. There is no such thing as a bad listing! I've heard Realtors say they wouldn't waste their time writing an over priced listing. I disagree with that position wholeheartedly! Taking over priced listings is not a waste of time.

Why?

Some over priced listings sell. Others end up being priced right at some time in the future when a Vendor/Seller becomes more serious. However, that's all beside the point. Provided the Vendor/Seller is fully aware the listing is over priced, having such a listing is certainly not a waste of time. Some of the best clients I've ever had, came as a result of having such an over priced listing.

One over priced listing that I carried for several years, illustrates their value better than anything else I can think of. My Vendor/Seller knew from the beginning his property was drastically over priced. He wasn't very motivated. He knew at the same time if he didn't have a ticket he couldn't win.

His circumstances changed a few years after I originally took the listing. At that point we priced it right and it sold quickly to a doctor. Subsequently, both the son and daughter of the purchaser bought homes from me. A few of their friends did also.

During the over priced period I had several sign calls who came for interviews and bought other properties. As well, during the same period, the over priced Vendor/Seller sent me several good referrals. They listed and/or purchased through me. This over priced listing made me thousands of dollars. And it continues to earn me money, as the Vendor/Seller still sends me a client occasionally. Over priced listings are not a waste of time. They can earn big money for those Realtors who know how to use them wisely!

NEVER CUT
YOUR COMMISSION

One of the plagues of the Real Estate business is the "Commission Cutter". It's a problem I wish I didn't have to contend with. Commission cutters are Realtors who have nothing else to offer! They're actually on their way out of the business although they don't know it. The fact is, that during my 25 years in the business, every company that has started on the basis of listing property at a commission lower than the going rate, has gone the way of the "Dodo Bird".

In all my years in the business, I have never found it necessary to cut a commission. Cutting commission is like eating popcorn. Once you start it's hard to stop! The best approach is not to start.

I don't cut commissions for anyone. Not for friends. Not for relatives. In fact, I can't understand why relatives or friends would expect me to give up my commission to sell their home. That's how I spend my time. That's how I earn my living! I don't expect them to forego any of their time at work, to contribute to my livelihood. Why should they expect it from me?

Furthermore, I've made it a policy over the years never to contribute my expertise as a Realtor to anyone, unless they pay for it.

When a Vendor/Seller asks me to cut my commission, I simply tell them that I've never cut my commission in 25 years in the business and I will not be starting on his listing.

I point out he is talking about my pay cheque. My pay cheque is like his. I count on it like he does. How would he feel if next pay day his boss asked him to take a cut in pay, yet work just as hard as he does now. But, that's exactly what he's asked me to do. Take a cut in pay. At the same time he wants me to work just as hard to sell his home.

Does this sound like good business to you?

If he asks me to cut my commission when we're negotiating an offer, I use the same approach. I ask how he would feel, if just an hour or two before the end of his pay period, when he had worked hard and just about completed his assigned job, the boss asked him if he would take less than he was supposed to get paid. He knows the answer. End of story.

PLAY BUSINESS
CARD POKER

I love it when a Vendor/Seller asks me to cut commission when we are doing a listing agreement. I often end up getting a higher commission after playing a little game with him. I call it "Business Card Poker". The odds are great! It's a very powerful sales tool. It proves the value of using visual aids in selling. And both the Vendor/Seller and I win!

Before we play the game though, I point out that Realtors are like anyone else earning a living. They notice the commission on each listing. If it's low they won't show the property. Why should they? Other properties are listed higher. They'll earn a Realtor a bigger pay cheque.

At this point I take out three business cards. I lay them on the table blank side up. I say to my Vendor, "Mr. Seller, I want you to help me settle this commission matter. Let's change roles here for a minute. You be the Realtor. I'll be the client".

"Now, I've just entered your office and I want to buy a home. You have three homes that would suit me. They are all identical. The price, the design, the condition and location are all the same. Just like these three business cards. One is listed at 3% which is less than half the going rate; another is listed at 7% which is the going rate; this last one is listed at 8%, having sort of a little bonus on it worth an extra $1000 to you, the Realtor. Which of these three homes are you going to sell me Mr. Seller?"

Given that illustration many Vendors/Sellers who suggest cutting commission will list with a bonus right on the spot. Others will phone later and ask you to increase the commission as they become more anxious to sell. None will want to list for less than the going rate.

I also explain that all things being equal, the law of averages dictates that his property will likely take 80 - 120 days to sell. To make the law of averages work more in his favor he has to price his home better than average, pay better than average commission, keep his home in better than average condition, and certainly have a better than average Realtor. All or any combination of the foregoing will help create a sale sooner.

Finally, I point out that in Real Estate like everything else in life you only get what you pay for. A commission cutter wouldn't ever be able to give him the good advice I just gave him — advice that will help him sell his home. **The fact of the matter is, that when Realtors become commission cutters they compromise their ability to advise their clients properly.**

"CHAPTER 20"

SERVICING LISTINGS

No matter where I go the question keeps coming up:

"How can you service so many listings?" The answer is really quite simple. My Vendors/Sellers don't make demands of me. Oh they used to! When I did things the way the AVERAGE Realtor does, I could never have dealt with over 50 listings.

My phone used to ring off the hook when I only had five or six Vendors/Sellers. They all wanted Ads and Open Houses. I'd run an Ad. They wouldn't like it. They'd call and complain. It was all negative! They all wanted Open Houses every Sunday. They were in control of my actions and my time! Talk about doing your job backwards!

That's how it used to be. Not anymore! Now I'm in control. I emphasize what I won't be doing. I don't have Vendors/Sellers calling to demand Advertising and Open Houses. They know I don't advertise properties. They know I don't hold public open houses. They call me about positive things. They had a Realtor show their home. They want to reduce the price. They want to raise the commission. I'm happy to oblige. It's all positive now. And I keep it that way.

If I find a negative Vendor/Seller has wandered into my family of happy, positive clients, I cancel his listing. As I said before, I don't need unhappy clients. No successful business person does.

KEEP PAPERWORK
AT A MINIMUM

I take all my listings for long terms. This cuts out the paperwork that would be involved for re-listing if they were written for short terms. It saves time. Time is money, when you keep busy at income generating activities.

If I wrote the more than 50 listings I carry for two months at a time instead of four months to a year, I'd spend up to six times as many hours per year writing re-listings or extensions than I do now. Assuming I'd have to spend only an hour on each listing each time I re-listed it, I could be wasting up to 300 hours yearly. It pays to write listings for as long a term as possible.

PROMOTE YOUR LISTINGS AT REALTOR OPEN HOUSES

I do sit Realtor Open Houses. I use them to SELL all my listings to other Realtors. When I sit a Realtor Open House I bring an album with me that features all my other listings in colour. In addition to sitting these myself, I also pay other Realtors to sit them for me.

When there are plenty of listings the turnout at Realtor Open Houses is usually less than when the supply of listings is low. This is because Realtors are spread out looking at a greater number of properties. In other words competition is keener.

In times like this you can do things to attract Realtors to see your listings. You can host a lunch for Realtors. You can get together with other Realtors who have listings in the area and have a progressive dinner. You can have a draw for a prize at each of several homes you hold open, with a grand prize draw at the last one, for those Realtors who've been to all of the homes you held open. You can host a Champagne Brunch for Realtors. You can give Lottery tickets to each Realtor who comes through, provided it's not illegal in your jurisdiction and your Vendor/Seller isn't against gambling.

OPPORTUNITY FOR PRICE REDUCTION

Participating with other Realtors in a progressive dinner often presents a great opportunity for having a discussion with your Vendor/Seller regarding a price reduction. If other homes featured on the dinner tour are priced better than his they'll have more appeal to the Realtors who come through. Is that what we want? Of course it isn't! We want ours to be the most appealing so we'll get the showings that follow. So, a price reduction may be the answer.

Many of my listings sell right after a Realtor Open House. In many cases, listings other than the one I sit on a given day sell. I promote all my listings to Realtors who come through the one I'm sitting. There isn't a better time to sell all your listings to other Realtors. No matter what the market is like, I spend a good portion of my promotional budget getting Realtors through my Realtor Open Houses.

When it comes to providing dinners, brunches or the like, you can often involve your Vendor/Seller as the cook. That leaves you free to act as host or hostess only. But that depends on you and your client. The same applies to the cost of such an occasion. You can pay for it yourself, share the cost with your Vendor/Seller, or have him pay the cost. There are several possibilities.

DISTRIBUTE FLYERS TO
REAL ESTATE OFFICES

You can promote your listings by doing flyers to all or various Real Estate offices. This a great way to draw attention to a price reduction, commission increase, or any other changes in your listing. I use flyers extensively with excellent results.

I also use flyers to encourage Realtors to attend a special function I may have at one or more properties being held Open for Realtors. Such functions might include a dinner, progressive dinner, brunch, or any other promotion aimed at generating more Realtor interest in a property.

MAKE SHOWINGS EASY
FOR OTHER REALTORS

The easier it is for me to show a listing the more likely I am to show it and sell it. If I have a difficult time making appointments with a Vendor/Seller, I won't show his home again unless I have to. Usually, if they are difficult to get along with at the showing stage, they're impossible to deal with when you have an offer. If I have to waste time fighting my way into a home, I'd rather show something else.

I explain to all my Vendors/Sellers, that if they want plenty of showings we have to make it easy for Realtors to show their home. I usually get keys from them so we can show their home if they're out. Then I leave keys at a friendly Real Estate Office in the area of the listing. That allows for easy pickup by other Realtors. I keep keys for all my listings in both my home and my car. In this way, I'm often able to accommodate Realtors who would like to make a showing after the Offices are closed.

I also try to get my Vendors/Sellers to keep a lockbox available with a set of keys in it. When they go out they can put it on their door. Then, if a Realtor wants to show the home when they're out he'll be able to do so. An alternative, is to leave a key with a neighbor for pickup by Realtors when they're not going to be home.

Making their home easy for Realtors to show can mean the difference between selling or not selling quickly, or even not selling at all. Homes that can be shown easily, are shown more often and sell faster, than those that are difficult for Realtors to show. I point out to my Vendors/Sellers that news travels fast in Real Estate circles. Both good news and bad news carry consequences of their own kind. We want the good kind.

Making listings easy to show is a major element in servicing listings. It saves time for me, my assistant, and my driver. It makes us all more efficient.

All the other basic and routine items required in servicing listings are carried out by my assistant. These are outlined in more detail in Chapter 24, 25, and 27 which deal with ASSISTANTS' DUTIES.

" C H A P T E R   21 "

HOW MANY LISTINGS
SHOULD A REALTOR CARRY?

I am frequently asked that question by new licensees

and veteran Realtors alike. How many listings should a Realtor carry? The answer can only be decided by determining how much money you want to earn. After that it's a matter of making the "law of averages" work for you. To do that you have to determine the sales to listings ratio in your area.

For example, in Calgary at the present time, Realtors who consistently carry seven well priced listings can be sure of one listing selling each month. Thus they can be sure of one commission cheque each month for every seven listings they carry. Throughout this current year I have carried an average of 65 listings. I have averaged eight listing commissions each month all year long.

Last year I had identical results carrying an average of 35 listings. In other words, last year I earned a listing commission each month for every four listings I carried as opposed to a commission for every seven this year. All you have to do to determine the optimum number of listings you should carry is this. Determine the listings to sales ratio for your area; and maintain your listing inventory at the level that will give you the annual income you want to earn.

There is also a ratio of Vendors/Sellers who REPURCHASE in your area versus those who do not. Some people sell and rent. Others move out of the area. For one reason or another they don't buy again. In my case, for every seven listing commissions I earn, I sell 4.5 of my Vendors/Sellers another home. Sometimes they buy one of my other listings. My average is 17 client transactions monthly. Out of this total 11.5 of my monthly client transactions come directly from my listings.

The five easiest sales I make each month are the five I make to those whose listings I've handled. They're prime clients. They know me and trust me. I know them. I know what they like and dislike. I know what they can afford. They know the City and all the amenities. The most important thing is, they represent a guaranteed commission.

GUARANTEE YOURSELF ANY INCOME YOU WANT

Since my average commission per client transaction is $3836, that translates to roughly 70% of my annual income or about $525,000.00. All I have to do is increase my active listings to increase my income. Any Realtor can guarantee himself or herself a given income, by consistently maintaining a listing inventory, relative to the sales to listing ratio for their particular area. If you can learn to be a "Good Lister" you'll last in this business. Always remember "Good Listers" are SLUMP PROOF! Listings guarantee income!

How many listings should a Realtor carry? "Enough To Guarantee You The Income You Want To Earn".

"C H A P T E R 22"

TECHNOLOGICAL ADVANCEMENTS

We're living in an era ruled by advanced technology.

In addition to the telephone, the two technological advancements that have revolutionized the way we do business more dramatically than all others, are the PERSONAL COMPUTER and the FAX machine.

GET YOURSELF
COMPUTERIZED NOW

The "Computer Age" is NOW! Its effects are here to stay! The Real Estate Industry, like dozens of other industries is being impacted more and more by computers. Every year more and more Real Estate Boards, MLS. Systems, Real Estate Offices, and individual Realtors are being computerized.

The day is rapidly approaching when every Realtor will need a computer of his own to remain competent, let alone competitive. In our area for example, those of us who utilize terminals or computers to access the local Real Estate Board, will know about new listings from several days to a week before those who do not.

We used to spend hour upon hour doing the research needed for putting together the Market Analyses we used to make listing presentations. Now, many of us can get more detailed and accurate Market Analyses in a few minutes, simply by accessing the computer at our local Board or MLS Office with our computers.

In many areas, we're also able to access Municipal Tax Information from City Hall or other Local Government computers. Some, can even access Title Information from public records stored in other Government computers. Credit information is available by accessing the files stored in the computer at the local Credit Bureau Offices. The list goes on and on.

INSTANTANEOUS INFORMATION

All this information is available instantaneously to those Realtors who have computers, in areas where it's accessible. Computers make it possible today for Realtors to be better informed, more efficient, and earn more money than our predecessors ever dreamed possible.

The consumer is being conditioned more and more to expect information instantly regarding every product that interests them. This trend will continue. When the generations presently attending our educational institutions emerge as consumers, they'll be demanding even more information and will expect to receive it even faster. We better be prepared to provide instant answers to their questions, or we simply won't get our share of their consumer dollar. It's that simple. I'm prepared to get my share. Now, how about you?

Even if your local Board or MLS System is not yet computerized, it's only a matter of time until they will be. In the meantime the proper use of a computer will make you far more efficient. And you'll be prepared to get your share of the disposable income of the consumer who will emerge from this High Tech Era.

My advice to career Realtors in this regard is simple: Get Computerized Now!

A PROGRAM FOR THE REALTOR IN THE FIELD

When I purchased my computer I couldn't find a Database Management Program which would make a Real Estate Salesperson more efficient. There were a multitude of programs available for the use of Corporate Executives and Sales Managers. But there simply wasn't anything of real value available for a Realtor in the field. In other words there was nothing available that was Real Estate specific.

I decided to solve that problem for myself.

I hired a Programmer who worked with me for several months. We developed our own package of programs. Several other Realtors purchased the package from me and this helped to defray some of my costs.

The package consists of a Client Program, A Referral Program, A Listing Activity Program and a Users Manual I had completed so my assistant would have no trouble operating the programs. I run my programs on both an IBM PC and a true IBM compatible PC.

The package was developed for my use as an individual Realtor. It's designed to require a minimal amount of time for inputting and updating. The purpose is to make me more efficient. The programs are totally complementary to the selling system outlined in this book.

Feel free to write me at the address listed at the end of the Preface at the front of this book, if you think I could make any useful suggestions that will help you get Computerized. I'll get back to you as soon as time permits.

THE FAX
REVOLUTION

When I wrote the first edition of this book in the mid 1980's, the FAX machine was just making its debut in the business world in general, and the Real Estate Business in particular. Although I'd purchased a FAX machine several years earlier I was able to use it only on a very limited basis. That was primarily with overseas clients, a few large law offices and a limited number of clients in large corporations, who had access to the company machine.

Gradually however the price of FAX machines came down, the speed at which documents could be transmitted quickened, and the quality of transmitted documents improved. These developments made the purchase and use of FAX machines both practical and economically viable. Nearly every firm, financial institution and law office I deal with today, has a FAX machine. Today nearly every department, in most corporations, has its own FAX machine. And now, many of my clients have FAX machines right in their homes. The result is, the FAX machine has had a revolutionary impact on virtually every type of business, including the Real Estate Business.

A FAX machine is relatively inexpensive to purchase. It's a real time and money saver. It pays for itself quickly.

Not only are they being used by most Real Estate Offices today, but they're quickly becoming an essential tool for the individual Realtor.

In addition to the FAX machine in my office, I've had a FAX machine permanently installed in my car, for several years now. It works off my cellular phone. It allows me to send and receive documents and information as I travel about the City in my car. I've sent and received offers and listings, to and from, such diverse places as Hong Kong, Sweden, Germany, Great Britain and from every corner of the U.S. and Canada from my car. I couldn't begin to count the miles and hours I've saved by having the FAX machine in my car.

There's another benefit from having a FAX machine with you at all times: **It serves as an on-the-spot photocopier.**

A COINCIDENTAL ILLUSTRATION

The day is fast approaching when nearly every client we deal with, will expect to receive information from us by FAX, even in their homes. And they'll be expecting to send us information by FAX from their homes as well! Coincidently, and to illustrate this point somewhat dramatically, as I was typing the previous sentence into the word processor, a document was coming over my FAX machine, which is located nearby. It reads as follows: "Marilyn, Saleslady from C21 whose business card appears above showed 8th Ave duplex today. Clients quite impressed according to tenants. Regards, Paul Schneider."

This FAX message was received shortly after midnight. Because I have a FAX machine my client was able to communicate this message to me AT HIS CONVENIENCE. Due to the lateness of the hour he would have been unable to do so if I didn't have a FAX nachine. Tomorrow, two things will happen as a result of this FAX message. My assistant will follow up on the showing with the Realtor and encourage an offer. My driver will send the Realtor a Thank You card in appreciation of showing our listing.

In my opinion, it won't be long before a FAX machine like a computer will be an absolute necessity for every Realtor, who hopes to remain competent and competitive, to say nothing about being efficient in the Real Estate Business.

My advice to Realtors: Join The FAX Revolution Now!

" C H A P T E R   23 "

HIRING
ASSISTANTS

Throughout this book there have been various

references to my assistant and my driver. Without my assistant, Suzanne, and my driver, Terry, it would be impossible to handle more than 50 listings and participate in more than 200 client transactions in a single year. Variously, it was mentioned that I delegate unproductive tasks to others. Included among the OTHERS are my full-time Assistant and full-time Driver. This chapter deals with some general questions regarding assistants. We'll deal more specifically with issues relating to both assistants and drivers in the following Chapters.

WHEN YOU HIT THE "TIME BARRIER" HIRE AN ASSISTANT

Since everyone works differently, it's difficult to determine at exactly what income level one should hire an assistant. It's also difficult to say at what point the position should become full-time as opposed to part-time. Another difficult thing to determine is when you should hire your own assistant, as opposed to sharing an assistant with another Realtor or Realtors. It's equally difficult to decide when to add a second assistant to your staff. And still more difficult to determine what exact function the second assistant should play.

Realtors from all over the continent come and meet with me. They desperately want to earn more but find they simply don't have the time to make any more sales. They tell me they're unable to get beyond their present income level. Their problem? They've hit the "Time Barrier!"

This problem can be resolved only by delegating those many unproductive tasks to others. When you reach the point where you could be busy full-time or most of the time, doing only direct income producing activities, it's time to hire an assistant. Delegate those unproductive activities to him or her. Only then can you break the "Time Barrier" and concentrate 100% of your time on direct income producing activities.

BASIC INCOME PRODUCING ACTIVITIES

I concentrate on four basic income producing activities. These are:

1) Initial Client Interviews — to acquire new purchaser clients. I generally set a day aside for this purpose every 7 to 10 days.

2) Listing Presentations — to get new listings.

3) Showing Properties — to obtain offers.

4) Presenting Offers.

Virtually everything else is handled by my assistant, my driver and others.

AN ASSISTANT
NOT A SECRETARY

The purpose of having an assistant is to make you more productive. The ultimate objective should be, to keep you booked up fully for two to three weeks in advance at all times. Your assistant is not, and should not be a secretary. Let your office provide the secretarial services the same as always. At least 50% to 60% of the time, your assistant will be out in the field doing those time consuming things you used to do. He or she should be an extension of you! And you're a Realtor — not a secretary!

REMUNERATION, QUALITIES
AND JOB DESCRIPTION

I pay both my assistant and my driver a straight salary plus an annual bonus. Neither their salaries nor bonuses are tied to my income in any way. I don't believe in that type of compensation arrangement for several reasons. First of all, I want to feel free NOT to deal with certain clients without having a decision of that kind affect someone else's livelihood. Secondly, I want to be able to take as much time off as I care to without it becoming an employer/employee concern that affects someone else financially.

Moreover, there is no reason why my assistants should suffer because I choose to give more away one year than another. For example, in 1985 and again this year, I've referred a lot of business to other Realtors so I could spend more time completing this book. And if Suzanne and

Terry's remunerations were tied to my income they'd suffer unfairly.

In addition to that, I believe in keeping compensation arrangements clear and simple. When you use this approach, you eliminate the potential for misunderstanding and conflict. The result is you have happier and more productive employees. AND A HAPPIER BOSS TOO!!

In order for an individual to be a good assistant several important qualities are necessary. The person has to be HIGHLY INTELLIGENT and able to relate well with all types of Realtors and Clients. They have to have a calm, cool personality and be able to adjust their plans readily and constantly. They should have an aptitude for business, be honest, sincere and really want the job.

Over the years, I've seen numerous Realtors hire assistants and end up disappointed and disilllusioned because it didn't work out. This usually happens for one or two main reasons.

The first has to do with remuneration. Obviously, if you're going to hire a highly intelligent person to do a job, they'll have to be remunerated accordingly. From my experience that tends to be in the same salary and bonus range as paralegals and personal corporate secretaries. If you're not prepared to offer an attractive remuneration package one of two things will happen. You'll either be unable to hire someone who is capable of being a good assistant, or if you are able to, they'll leave your employment as soon as a better opportunity presents itself.

The other main reason for assistants not working out has to do with the Realtor not letting go. For some reason, after hiring an assistant, Realtors often fail to pass on those responsibilities that should be delegated to the assistant. I recently had a Realtor visit me. He was concerned, he said, because he couldn't seem to keep people in his employ who were properly qualified and whom he paid well. When he told me he still put sold stickers on signs and delivered feature sheets to his Vendors/Sellers himself, the reason was obvious. In fact, I was hard pressed to find anything his assistant did for him, except take messages. When Realtors fail to let go and delegate all non-income producing tasks to their assistants, the result is twofold. The Realtor is no more efficient or effective than before hiring an assistant, and invariably, the assistant leaves because they feel useless, bored and unchallenged by the job.

As for the job description, it will vary from individual to individual, from office to office, and from region to region because functions, rules and laws differ. The next four Chapters deal with many of the duties an assistant can perform. The first one (Chapter 24) is my description of what Suzanne's job entails. The second one (Chapter 25) is Suzanne's own description of her job as my assistant. These two Chapters will assist you in preparing a job description for your own assistant. And Chapters 26 and 27 deal similarly with my description and Terry's own description of his job as my driver.

ASSISTANTS'
DUTIES

You might wonder just what an Assistant to a Realtor

would do. The following is a partial list of duties Suzanne performs for me.

LISTING
PRESENTATIONS

Usually before a listing is acquired a Listing Presentation is made. This normally involves a "Market Analysis" of some sort. Our local MLS system is computerized. We obtain our "Market Analyses" through the computer.

Like manually prepared ones, computer prepared analyses provide lists of active listings, expired listings, and sold listings and give an average price for the property. The lists show the extras or lack of same for each property. A "Market Analysis" done manually would include all the same information. Based on that information you can have an intelligent conversation with a prospective Vendor/Seller, about the value of his property.

When I have a Listing Presentation to make, my assistant runs the computerized "Market Analysis". She highlights all the comparables. She puts it in a presentation folder, together with my Personal Brochure, the latest newspaper or magazine article about me, Sold stickers and any other appropriate or applicable promotional material. I simply pick it up and take it with me to do my presentation.

SERVICING
LISTINGS

Once a listing is obtained my assistant services it. All I do is get the contract signed and get on to the next appointment.

The next day my assistant meets the Vendor/Seller. At that meeting, she arranges for a Realtor open house and discusses how they can make the home more appealing for showings. She measures the inside and outside of the home. She has the Vendor/Seller write down all the features on a form we provide for that purpose. She arranges for the photographer to take coloured pictures. These are for the feature sheets and albums we use to promote ALL my listings to other Realtors, at Realtor Open Houses.

My assistant has extra keys cut and a combination lockbox placed on the property so Realtors can show the home easily. She fills out the computer forms and turns the listing into the office.

She arranges to have information sheets and feature sheets prepared by the office. Upon completion she delivers them to the Vendor/Seller. They're left at the home to assist Realtors who show the listing. She orders the sign company to put up the sign. She arranges for Realtor Open Houses with the Real Estate Board.

Neighbourhood canvass cards are filled out. She either does the canvass of 75 homes in the area herself, or makes arrangements to have it done by my driver or someone else immediately. She ensures flyers are drafted up and delivered to my own and other Real Estate offices regularly — throughout the term of the listing. She follows up showings by other Realtors when the Vendor/Seller calls to let us know the home was shown.

Suzanne arranges for lawns to be cut and driveways and sidewalks cleaned when necessary. She replenishes information and feature sheets as the listing price or other changes are made, or they get used up. She ensures "Thank You" post cards are sent to every Realtor who shows our Listings. She develops excellent rapport with every Vendor/Seller. She makes them feel as if we're always working just for them. She's an extension of me.

PROPERTY
<u>SHOWINGS</u>

When I show property to prospective Purchasers, or other Realtors show my listings to their prospective Purchasers, an offer may develop. If you want your listings shown, you have to make it EASY for other Realtors to show them. Making sure my listings are easy to show is also one of my assistant's duties.

We make sure that we have keys for every listing if possible. We keep a set at the office, at home, in my car, and at a friendly Real Estate office in the area of the listing, for easy pickup by Realtors. We even send keys by courier to other Realtors if they're unable to pick them up.

My assistant makes sure Realtors are able to show my listings when they want to. She sees they get the keys, that the keys are returned, and she makes sure if necessary, that Realtors get appointments to show my listings when they want to.

For my own showings she arranges all the appointments with owners or Realtors as required. She either picks up keys for me or has them picked up by my driver. She plans out the route my driver will follow. She arranges to have keys I use returned by my driver or by some other means.

We've worked together long enough now, that I simply give Suzanne a few guidelines and she makes appointments on suitable property with no trouble at all. She arranges for clients to be picked up at their home, hotel or airport by my driver and brought to my office.

ACCEPTED
OFFERS

When an offer has been accepted I get out of the picture. My assistant takes over. Suzanne arranges to have the courier service certify the cheque. She delivers copies of the certified cheque to my office or to other Realtors, or vice-versa, depending on whether it was my listing that sold or if I sold someone else's listing.

She gathers and fills out all the conveyancing information, such as the Lawyers names, addresses, etc. She distributes copies to all concerned. She has my driver fill out 75 neighbourhood canvass cards and canvass the neighbourhood immediately or has someone else do it. She ensures that the "Conditionally Sold" and "Sold" stickers are put on the sign. She arranges for the sign to be taken down on closing.

She coordinates things with lawyers offices and stays on top of having "Conditions" or "Subject To's" waived. She obtains and distributes copies of such waivers to all concerned. She assists purchasers with any measuring they have to do prior to closing.

If it's my listing that sold she has Key Lockboxes removed if we had a Lockbox on the home. If the home is vacant she checks it periodically till possession. She makes a final inspection with the purchaser prior to "closing" when necessary.

TRANSACTION CLOSINGS

Suzanne stays on top of closings and makes sure keys are available for the purchaser. When approval is given to release keys she arranges to have them delivered or picked up as may be required.

TELEPHONE CALLS

Suzanne handles all telephone calls from Realtors and most calls from Lawyers. When Realtors want to show my listings they phone Suzanne. She looks after the arrangements and promotes my other listings to them.

Most of the calls from Vendors/Sellers are also handled by Suzanne. They get to know her. They feel comfortable and well looked after by her. When they have showings by other Realtors they report to Suzanne. She follows up with the Realtors and reports back. When owners decide on a price reduction she reports it to the MLS Board. She does the same with mortgage changes, payment changes, property tax changes and/or corrections.

COMPUTER IN-PUTS AND PRINT-OUTS

I am a highly computerized person. A major part of both my assistant's and my driver's duties are computer related.

Every morning Suzanne spends the first 1 to 2 hours inputting the computer. She then provides me with up-to-date reports containing all the latest information I need. Since I work with a list of about 150-220 prospects at all times this list changes rapidly. It must be constantly updated. The same applies to my Listing Activity Report and Referral Reports.

Three times each week I receive new computer print-outs to keep me up to date. My assistant has to be familiar with and capable of inputting and running the computer programs for me.

ANOTHER
PERSPECTIVE

The foregoing is a description, as I see it, of many of the duties my assistant performs for me on a regular basis. Numerous Realtors have had their newly hired or prospective assistants come and spend a day with Suzanne. They wanted them to see first hand what it is that Realtor assistants do. Invariably the assistants had read this Chapter of this book before coming. They were aware of my perspective of what Suzanne does for me. But after meeting and spending time with Suzanne they had a different and even better perspective of what the job entailed.

Several suggested that when we did the next printing of CHAMPIONSHIP SELLING we should include Suzanne's description as well as mine. They felt that when Realtors gave the book to new or prospective assistant employees, it would be extremely beneficial for them to see both the employer and employee perspectives of the job. Consequently when I was preparing for this printing of the book I asked both my assistant Suzanne, and my driver Terry, to write out their own "Job Descriptions". The next Chapter contains Suzanne's own description of her job as my unlicensed assistant. As mentioned earlier, Chapter 27 contains Terry's own description of his job as my driver-assistant.

" C H A P T E R   25 "

MY JOB DESCRIPTION:
BY SUZANNE STARRIE

The main responsibilities of a Realtor Assistant is to

relieve the Realtor of all tasks not requiring direct client contact. Specific responsibilities and requirements would include the following.

PREPARATION OF DOCUMENTATION

Preparing documentation for presentations, interviews and market analyses and could include:

a) Assembling a package for the client to include personal information on the Realtor;

b) Retrieving appropriate data from the Real Estate Board (ours is accessible through our computer) to allow the Realtor to do an accurate pricing of a property;

c) Creating a supply of pertinent information, articles, maps, brochures etc., on the Realtor, the City and surrounding areas or Real Estate in general, that would be of interest to the client as part of an interview or presentation package.

d) Sending appropriate follow-up and thank-you letters to clients and others after doing Market Analyses and other presentations. (These are usually "stored on hand" in our computer).

PROCESSING
LISTINGS

Once the Realtor has obtained a listing, the assistant would follow up by:

a) Arranging with the Vendor/Seller, to go to the property the next day in order to:

   — establish contact with the Vendor/Seller or tenants
   — make detailed notes on the property
   — measure the inside and outside of the home
   — have Vendor/Seller fill out "Feature Sheet Preparation Forms" noting all the features of the property
   — arrange a Realtor open house
   — arrange a suitable time for the photographer to take coloured photos for the feature sheets and the Realtor's album;

b) Complete and submit listing forms to the Real Estate Board;

c) Arrange with the photographer to have coloured pictures taken of the exterior of the home and, when appropriate, the interior and surrounding areas;

d) Arrange to have a "For Sale" sign put up on the property;

e) Have keys cut; place a key lockbox on the home and instruct the occupant in its use, and when not allowed to place a lockbox on the home arrange with a friendly Real Estate office in the area of the listing to have keys left there for pick up by Realtors who want to show the home; give set of keys to driver to keep in car and keep set at office as well;

f) Have information and feature sheets prepared and delivered to the home;

g) Arrange to have neighbourhood canvass done.

POST LISTING
SERVICES

After initial processing of a listing, the following servicing is required:

a) Maintaining communication and rapport with the owners by following up on all showings and reporting back to them;

b) Dealing promptly and tactfully with any problems or concerns that may arise for the Vendor/Seller in regard to showings;

c) Replenishing information and feature sheets as necessary;

d) Keeping the Realtor informed of all activity;

e) Arranging for upkeep or repairs of vacant properties when necessary;

f) Correcting and updating information when needed.

PROCESSING OFFERS

Once an offer has been accepted the assistant:

a) Arranges to either have the deposit cheque certified (if the deposit is payable to our company) or ensures that a copy of the certified cheque is obtained from the cooperating Realtor (if the deposit is made payable to the cooperating company). If the cheque is made payable to our company then we ensure that a copy of the certified cheque is provided to the cooperating Realtor;

b) Ensures that copies of the agreement and cheque are delivered to all appropriate parties;

c) Obtain data necessary to complete conveyancing forms, such as names, addresses and phone numbers of the lawyers/attorneys, the Vendor/Seller and purchaser, and all relevant information regarding the Realtors involved, so that upon completion commission and referral payments can be paid promptly to them.

Following up to completion of the purchase may include:

a) Keeping track of dates for removal of "conditions" or "subject to's" and ensuring all parties receive copies of waivers when completed and signed;

b) Ensuring that lawyers/attorneys for all parties receive all additional documents executed by the parties;

c) Assisting the purchaser in obtaining measurements, survey certificates or information that may be required;

d) Arranging a pre-closing inspection of the property;

e) Arranging for the purchaser to obtain the keys on closing;

f) Ensuring commission cheques are collected and recorded.

In addition, when the sale involves one of our own listings it is necessary to:

a) Upon acceptance of an offer, arrange to have "C/S" (conditionally sold) or "SOLD" stickers put on the sign. In the case of a "C/S" have "SOLD" stickers put on when the conditions have been waived;

b) Arrange an appointment for a mortgage appraisal to be done if required by the purchaser;

c) Remove the key lockbox from the property;

d) Arrange to have a neighbourhood canvass done;

e) Arrange to have the sign removed at closing.

SETTING UP
<u>APPOINTMENTS</u>

A task that is very time-consuming, and one that can be done by the assistant, is that of setting up appointments for the Realtor to show properties to a client. The assistant should be able to:

a) Prepare lists of active listings appropriate for the client and select suitable properties for viewing;

b) Plot the most efficient route and arrange appointments accordingly;

c) Supply copies of scheduled appointments to the Realtor (and driver) with instructions for access to each property and the name and phone number of a contact person to call in the event that an appointment has to be changed or cancelled or there is some other problem with access;

d) Prepare information sheets on any selected properties not in the current MLS catalogue (e.g. computer print-outs from the Real Estate Board or info obtained from the listing Realtor on an Exclusive Listing).

Occasionally it will be necessary to conduct an ongoing search for appropriate active listings for a particular client. In this case, daily checking on new listings is required, so the Realtor will be aware as soon as possible of anything that may be of interest to that client.

MAINTAINING
COMMUNICATIONS

Maintaining communications is a vital part of the Real Estate business. The telephone is the major tool here. A clear voice and a pleasant and efficient manner are musts!! The idea of speaking with a Realtor's Assistant is relatively new, and having a confident and knowledgeable attitude will put most people, Realtors and the general public alike, at ease and feeling comfortable dealing with you.

Having the assistant screen as many calls as possible will save the Realtor enormous amounts of time. The assistant should:

a) Handle most calls leaving the Realtor free to concentrate on income producing activities such as doing Market Analyses, listing property, showing property and presenting offers. In particular the assistant should handle all calls relating to:

— inquiries from lawyers acting for your Vendor/ Seller or purchaser
— requests for appointments to show listings
— requests from other Realtors for information on listings
— comments, complaints or inquiries from Vendors/ Sellers (here's where the rapport that you've already established really comes in handy!);

b) When out of the office, make arrangements for calls to be taken by the telephone answering service, pick up messages frequently and return calls promptly.

Another important communications tool is the follow-up letter. The assistant should send out:

a) Appropriate letters to prospects with whom the Realtor had initial contact, either in person or by phone, and who wish to have further information;

b) Thank-yous to prospective clients who have had the Realtor do a market analysis on their home;

c) Thank-yous to former clients who have referred friends or colleagues to the Realtor;

d) Thank-yous to other Realtors who've referred clients to us;

e) Cards to other Realtors to say Thank You for showing our listings or for any other nice gesture they've made to us.

Flyers can be an efficient method of communication — to make other Realtors aware of your listings. Preparing and delivering brief, eye-catching leaflets regularly, ensures that everyone is aware of your special offerings and your Realtor stays foremost in their minds.

Screening of incoming mail by the assistant will not only save the Realtor time that might be wasted on nonessential (i.e. non-client contact) business, but allows the assistant to keep up on things that might otherwise have been missed had she/he (I'm sure Terry, Marilyn's driver would have said he/she here) not had access to the mail.

The Realtor's PERSONAL DIARY is an essential means of communication with the assistant. Checking it over at the start of each day allows the assistant to be aware of the day's schedule and provides the assistant with any new information that should be recorded and entered into the computer.

THE KEY TO EFFICIENT OPERATION

The key to an efficient operation is up-to-date and accurate (computer) files. In this regard:

a) The assistant should set aside time each day to collect any new information and create new files or add to existing ones as needed;

b) It's convenient for both the Realtor and assistant to have print-outs of the current records, so whenever more information is added new copies should be printed;

c) Each week, reminder lists should be prepared for pending closings, waivers of "conditions or "suject-tos", expiring listings and client callbacks;

d) At the end of each month, month-end reports should be prepared — a good safeguard against omissions as well as serving as ongoing statistical records.

OFFICE MANAGEMENT

The amount of office management required will vary according to each situation. When the office in which the assistant works is separate from the main Real Estate office, it's necessary to maintain a general office as follows:

a) Periodic inventory review to ensure adequate supplies of all office materials, ordering replacements as necessary;

b) Ensuring regular maintenance and servicing of office equipment such as computers, copiers, FAX machines, etc.;

c) Maintaining a petty cash fund for minor purchases;

d) Maintaining adequate supplies of MLS forms, brochures, cards, etc. and keeping the Realtor's briefcase and car supplied with these items;

e) Maintaining daily contact with the main Real Estate office, likely stopping in to drop off and pick up documents and other information.

A CAR IS
<u>ESSENTIAL</u>

Just as the Realtor must have a reliable car, so must the assistant. The assistant should expect to spend from one to four hours per day out of the office, running errands, servicing listings, etc. Some points regarding the use of the car are as follows:

a) Accurate records of gas consumption and mileage should be kept for reimbursement and/or tax purposes;

b) Good navigational skills are a must — keep good up-to-date maps handy at all times;

c) It's advisable to have some basic supplies stored in the car:

— spare tape measure
— pads of paper for notes
— pens, pencils (for when it's too cold for pens to write)
— extra maps
— the Realtor's personal brochures
— envelopes in two or three sizes
— business cards
— "C/S" and "SOLD" stickers
— window signs
— car expense record book

TAKE OFF THE PRESSURE

In general the assistant should take the pressure off the Realtor, allowing him/her more time and energy to devote to productive income generating activities. Just knowing that all the above mentioned, time consuming tasks are well in hand, will give the Realtor the peace of mind necessary to conduct her/his business to the best of their ability. And having their Realtor working, at the peak of their performance, provides the assistant with the satisfaction of a job well done.

" C H A P T E R 26 "

HIRING A
DRIVER

Why would a Realtor have a driver? Since I employ

a driver full time, I get to answer this question frequently. And it's a question with several answers.

First of all, I want to make it clear that no one should hire a driver, simply because they think it's so impressive they'll get business just because of it. I've never had anyone deal with me for that reason. In fact, the vast majority of clients couldn't care less.

TWO GOOD REASONS
FOR HIRING A DRIVER

There are two good reasons for hiring a driver. The first is related to Time Management. When you've reached the point where you and your Assistant together, can no longer handle the volume without additional help, perhaps a driver is the answer.

I was at this point when I first hired a driver. My assistant was no longer able to keep up with what had to be done. Neighbourhood canvasses were not being done promptly. We were constantly behind. Much of the work should have been done a whole lot sooner. We were at the point where inefficiency was taking over again. We had hit the "Time Barrier" for the second time!

This brings us to the second good reason for hiring a driver. Among other things, I wasn't getting my phone calls returned as promptly as I should have been. I came home every day Tired and Stressed!

We took a serious look at how to correct both these problems. We decided a driver was the answer. That's proved to be a wise decision.

I now get much more done while travelling. Since I have a Cellular Car Phone my calls are always returned promptly. I don't have to worry about traffic as I did when driving myself. Having a car phone and driver in effect allows me to do my desk work as we travel around the City. I am able to accomplish much more — by simply making more effective use of my time.

CLIENTS AND NEEDS
GET MORE ATTENTION

Instead of operating my automobile I can now study a market analysis while travelling to a listing presentation. Because of this, I'm able to make a far better presentation. When showing homes to purchasers I can sell them faster because I can give 100% of my time to them. I can deal with their questions and concerns instead of traffic signs, speed limits, school children and the like.

When I'm doing a listing presentation, the Vendors/ Sellers often notice there is someone in the car. When they ask me who it is I tell them it's my driver. They want to invite him in. I explain that this is not possible. He's out there working. His job is taking phone calls, returning phone calls and making appointments for other Realtors to show my listings. He may even leave to drop keys off to other Realtors and come back to pick me up. I explain that after we list their home, he'll be doing similar things to aid in marketing their property.

As soon as the Vendor agrees to write up the listing I excuse myself to make a phone call. I phone my driver, Terry, and tell him. He immediately fills out 50 canvass cards and does the neighbourhood canvass. On many occasions, the Vendor/Seller not being aware of who I phoned will ask when we actually start work on selling his home. I tell him we already started as my driver at that very moment is out canvassing the neighbourhood. Needless to say they're always impressed. And they never say, "We don't want a "For Sale" sign because we don't want the neighbours to know we're selling"!

Many of the more elementary tasks my assistant once handled are now the responsibility of my driver. He does all the neighbourhood canvasses. He picks up keys; helps make appointments for me to show property; delivers flyers promoting my listings to other offices; returns keys; picks clients up and returns them home. He keeps the car clean and maintains supplies, copies of my listings and spare keys for my listings in the car. He lays out the route we follow to show property to clients after consulting with my assistant.

My driver takes his instructions primarily from my assistant whose overall responsibility is to keep me prepared and organized. While waiting in the car for me to finish a listing presentation or an offer presentation, Terry designs flyers promoting our listings, on the computer in the car. These will be run off later and delivered to other Real Estate offices. Late at night when he's waiting he writes out "Thank You" cards. He addresses them to Realtors who have shown our listings or who have recently done something nice for us. During the day when he's waiting he delivers flyers promoting my listings, to Real Estate offices in the area we are in.

Terry sends and receives fax communications, and makes photocopies as needed, using the fax machine I've had permanently installed in the car.

He meets out of town clients at the airport and brings them to my office. In the past, this was a mammoth time waster which often killed a half day.

There are two major benefits from having a driver if you're extremely busy. Firstly, having a driver aids in the better management of one's Time. Secondly, it goes a long way towards eliminating Stress. However, unless you're extremely busy — booked solidly at all times for at least two weeks in advance — you certainly don't need a driver.

The foregoing represents my description of the tasks my driver does for me. As I mentioned in an earlier Chapter, as a result of the suggestion having been made by several Realtors' assistants who came to spend time with Suzanne, I asked both her and my driver to prepare their version of their job descriptions for me, for inclusion in this printing of CHAMPIONSHIP SELLING. The next Chapter is Terry's own description of his job as my driver-assistant.

" C H A P T E R 27 "

MY JOB DESCRIPTION: BY TERRY SHAW

My duties as a Realtor's driver-assistant fall into several

general categories as follows:

1. Operate limousine-type vehicle for all travel during and between appointments.

2. Care and servicing of vehicle to keep it in good safe working condition and appearance.

3. Performance of Realtor assistant duties such as preparation and distribution of promotional material, access to property and miscellaneous chores associated with listing and selling property.

These duties are addressed in more specific detail below.

VEHICLE OPERATION

Careful driving in all weather and traffic conditions with attention to the safety and comfort of all passengers. An intimate knowledge of the City and environs is required; and the ability to maintain strict timing is essential. A Realtor must always be on time, and a good driver should endeavour to assist in this aim. Attention to detail such as assisting passengers when entering and leaving the vehicle is important, and can be a valuable means of providing client satisfaction. A daily business log of trips and associated expenses is kept for tax purposes.

VEHICLE CARE
AND SERVICING

Regular maintenance in accordance with established schedules will ensure long life to an expensive automobile. Small problems should be rectified before serious conditions result. Such things as daily washing and interior vacuuming together with clean windows will impress and assist clients.

REALTOR
ASSISTANCE

This takes a number of different forms but generally can be summed up as follows:

a) Preparation and distribution of promotional flyers on property listings. Broad guidelines are received and flyers are computer produced and photocopied in sufficient quantity to allow delivery to individual Realtors across the City.

b) Assistance in providing access to our listings for other Realtors.

c) Assistance in providing directional signs outside the city limits and fixation of "conditional" and "sold" stickers on "for sale" signs.

d) Delivery and pickup of documentation regarding sales and listings, and delivery of property information and special features sheets to our Vendors/Sellers.

e) Canvassing potential clients in the vicinity of all "sold" and "listed" properties. Whenever possible, time is taken to notify residents of their new neighbours in the case of a sale, or to announce the availability of a listing in case friends of existing residents wish to relocate to the area. This personal contact dispels the impression that we are merely stuffing their mailbox with junk literature. Canvass material consists of the Realtor's personal brochure together with a card which indicates the address and name of new neighbours or new listing.

f) Preparation and mailing of "thank you" and "congratulatory" postcards to Realtors and others who do something nice for us, who show our listings or who achieve sales awards, recognition or other distinction.

MISCELLANEOUS TASKS

Several miscellaneous tasks are undertaken as follows:

a) Assistance in maintaining, in the car and Realtor's briefcase, a stock of office supplies such as letterhead, computer paper, open house signs for Realtor open houses, promotional material, fax paper, printer ink cartridges, etc. All these supplies are controlled as to location, availability and re-supply.

b) Assistance at Realtor "open houses" such as placement of directional signs and catering requirements if food and/or refreshments are served.

c) Operate cellular car phone regarding important messages or assistance to other Realtors when Realtor is absent from car or is occupied with clients.

d) Operate computer in car to:

    (i) obtain spontaneous information from Real Estate Board on properties spotted with "for sale" signs that are not yet in the catalogue, and;

    (ii) obtain spontaneous information as required from our own computerized records, and;

    (iii) design promotional flyers regarding our existing listings for later printing and distribution to Real Estate offices.

e) Operate FAX machine in car to send, receive and photocopy documents as needed.

APPORTIONMENT
OF TIME

An average of 9 hours per day, six days per week is worked. A rough apportionment of time spent on various duties would be as follows:

Vehicle operation and maintainance 50%

Preparation and distribution of
promotional material 25%

Tasks associated with sales and listings 15%

Miscellaneous tasks 10%

Total 100%

" C H A P T E R 28 "

YOU NEED ALL THE
ESSENTIAL TOOLS

In the sales business we spend a lot of time in our

cars. My Cellular Mobile Phone is one of the best investments I've ever made. It makes my driving time doubly productive. I can return and make telephone calls as I travel from one place to another.

For those of you who are not familiar with this Phone, it assures total privacy and features direct dialing from your car. It's one of the tools of my trade that I consider essential.

I also provide a portable cellular telephone to my assistant. This too, I consider essential. You can't expect employees to do a superb job for you, if you don't provide them with proper equipment.

I can't emphasize enough, that in order to be successful you have to have ALL the essential tools, or you'll lose deals.

Among the other tools that I consider essential are my personal computers, FAX machines and associated equipment. When those presently occupying our educational institutions emerge as consumers, I'm going to be prepared to meet their demands for instant information so I can get my share of their consumer dollar. That's why I consider my computers and FAX machines essential tools of my trade.

Good personal promotion material is also essential. For more on this subject see Chapter 30.

Don't lose $2500 trying to save $100 that should have been spent on photos, catalogues, maps or other essentials.

DON'T MISUSE
THE ESSENTIAL TOOLS

Misuse of the essential tools of our Profession is as much a cause of failure as their nonuse. An experience I had shortly after I entered the Real Estate Sales Profession illustrates this point quite clearly.

Although this story relates to my misuse of the telephone the principle could just as easily apply to any of the other essential tools.

Like many other new salespeople I was using the telephone for the wrong purpose without realizing it. I was doing telephone canvassing every day without much success. An old pro who always had plenty of appointments took me aside and gave me a lecture that I've never forgotten. It was one of the most valuable sales lessons I've ever learned. **He said, "I've been watching you use the telephone young lady, and you're going about it all the wrong way. If you want a client to sign a contract you have to put a pen in his hand instead of a receiver in his ear. In the sales business the telephone should be used for only two purposes. First it should be used to make appointments. Secondly it should be used to tell your spouse what time you'll be home for dinner. Any other use of the telephone by a salesperson during working hours should be seriously questioned."**

As my career progressed I came to realize the validity of the advice my old friend gave me. Even though the advice appears to be somewhat narrow and also extreme, I've probably obtained more listings and sales over the years because of it than anything else I've learned. The phone is used by every Realtor for many other purposes every day of the year. And, it will continue to be that way.

But, if we do as my old friend suggested, and question the necessity of all the other purposes we use the phone for, we can't help but be more productive as a result. And I know from experience, that we'd all have more appointments, if every time we picked up the receiver we said to ourselves, **"I'm picking this up to get an appointment."**

Somehow, telling our spouses what time we'll be home for dinner has never seemed as important to me as some of the other uses I've found for my telephone over the years. I know it wasn't that important to my old friend either. I found out later he never called his spouse about dinner. You see, he was a bachelor who lived by himself. And a great teacher!

" C H A P T E R 29 "

THE VALUE OF
LEISURE TIME

Time Management also means ensuring you have plenty

of leisure time for yourself and your family. Never discount the value of leisure time. It can play a critical role in helping you reach your goals.

Salespeople sell best when they're excited, motivated, and enthusiastic. Anyone who works 60 - 70 hours weekly with no time off is doing something wrong. Even super sales people who keep their nose to the grindstone seven days a week, week in and week out, become dull without an appropriate amount of leisure time and activities.

To remain vital and dynamic, spend a balanced portion of your time at leisurely and recreational activities. This is critical to maintaining a healthy, vibrant outlook on life. To remain sharp, physically and mentally alert, you have to take time off and relax! Everyone functions best when they're rested and recharged.

EXCLUDE NONESSENTIAL ACTIVITIES

To become an effective time manager you'll have to eliminate nonessential activities from your schedule. Your life will no longer be cluttered by unproductive events. Add up all the wasted hours you spend at non-income producing meetings. Convert the majority of them into income producing activities. You'll have time left for an afternoon of golf, a nice romantic dinner out, or a Las Vegas weekend. You'll come back rested, excited, and enthusiastic about life and your career.

I take one full day off per week. In addition I take every Tuesday afternoon off to paint. I also take EVERY MORN-ING off, — that's right EVERY MORNING as I don't start work until noon each day — to relax, read or listen to a motivational tape and generally get my head straight for the balance of the day. Every five to six weeks I go away for four to seven days. I take several additional longer holidays each year. In fact, in 1989 I took more time off than I worked and still earned in excess of $700,000. These various recharges keep my attitude healthy, which in turn make sales easier, which in turn help me reach my goals and earn more money.

" C H A P T E R 30 "

PERSONAL
PROMOTION

My clients are always amazed at the reception I get

from other Realtor's Vendors/Sellers when we're looking at property. They often run over when we're leaving and say, "You're the lady we've read so much about. Let me shake your hand." Others say, "Even if you don't sell our house I'm just so honoured you've shown it." When these things happen and they do regularly, I know I'm doing something right! My "Personal Promotion" program is working!!

Calgary is a City of some 650,000 people. Yet, in all areas of the City, Vendors/Sellers whom I've never seen before, know of me. They've read articles about me in newspapers or magazines; seen me on television interviews; heard me on radio interviews; read ads about me in magazines and newspapers; received promotional material about me at their door; picked up my personal brochure in a hotel, restaurant or office; or heard of me from friends, relatives or acquaintances. Often their own Realtor has told them about me and my achievements when they made the appointment for us.

PROMOTE YOURSELF — DON'T ADVERTISE PROPERTY

In earlier chapters I mentioned that I do not advertise properties in the newspapers. That's true. I don't. However, I do spend about 9% of my income, roughly $60,000.00 per year, on Personal Promotion. If I spent the same amount advertising properties in newspapers no one would even know I existed. They'd know my company better perhaps, but not me. I'd be dealing with poor quality prospects rather than top quality clients. I could never earn the kind of money I do now.

Every envelope you send out should contain some Personal Promotion material. When an envelope leaves my office, it always contains at least one item with my picture and a little something about me. My Personal Brochure goes to law offices, banks, trust companies, Realtors and anyone else who receives an envelope from me. Even my creditors get one when I pay my bills.

PERSONALIZE
EVERYTHING

Every piece of material that I send out including my letterhead is personalized. Everything has my picture on it. The emphasis is on me. It's not on the company.

I work from my home. My office is there. All my promotional material, including For Sale signs, contain only my phone number and not that of the company I'm licensed with. My calls come to me directly. I have my own answering service. We receive between 60 and 80 calls per day. Very, very seldom does the company get a phone call for me from the general public. They do get calls from other Realtors. These are referred to my number.

TELL YOUR CLIENTS, THE PRESS AND YOUR PEERS

When I do my two annual promotions to my clients I enclose a letter promoting myself. I thank them for their referrals. I solicit more referrals from them. I update them on my latest accomplishments. My client list numbers over 800. Theoretically this means that twice each year, there are some 800 families out there who tell my story to their friends, relatives, and acquaintances. Because of the large number of referrals I get from former clients, I know a great many of them do just that.

I keep members of the Business Press informed of my accomplishments. I send them updated copies of my Personal Brochures each year. I include members of the business press in my promotions. On the other hand, I never ask or pressure them to write about me. I simply make the facts available to them.

It's prudent indeed, to make your peers aware of your accomplishments. My Personal Brochure is received by more than 12,000 Realtors locally, nationally, and internationally each year. Realtors familiar with my accomplishments talk to other Realtors about me. Their friends in the business often send me referrals, or write, or call me for advice or assistance.

I always make time for Realtors or other salespeople wanting a bit of help. In the past, when I was still working mornings, when I'd sit a Realtor Open House, I'd usually invite someone looking for advice or assistance to spend the morning with me. Now, I have them come to my office for a visit. I find this is time well spent. The time I spend with other Realtors wins me their respect and good-

will — something that no amount of advertising can purchase. If for some reason they leave the business they refer
their friends to me when they need a Realtor. In fact, several
former Realtors are among my more prolific referral
sources.

Since students and new licensees often call me, I know
that I am cited as an example at Real Estate Courses run
by our local board, at courses run by other boards, and
at various sales seminars sponsored by other groups.

People have gone out of their way to deal with me
because my name was mentioned at seminars sponsored
by their company or professional organization. This has
happened with Life Insurance Salespeople, Investment
Dealers, and a person selling Construction Equipment not
to mention several others. Those from other sales fields
send me clients because they've read or heard about me.

All of the foregoing indicates that my Personal Promotion program is effective. It is bringing satisfactory results.

GO FIRST CLASS AND BE CONSISTENT

There are a few important points that need to be made
regarding Personal Promotion. First and foremost, anything
and everything you hand out to the public should be first
class material. The quality and how you present it, is far
more important than the quantity. In other words it is far
better to make do with one item that looks first class than
to have two or three items that are mediocre.

It is also advisable to be consistent so people identify with you. I use the same gifts every year for my two major promotions. All of my promotional material is done in burgundy with full colour photos of myself. Over the years people have come to identify with my promotional gifts and my burgundy material.

I'm not suggesting in any way that all promotional material has to be done in full four or five colour process, in order to be first class. I've seen material in full colour that looked awful. I've also seen material done in black and white that looked first class.

If you want material to look first class you should expect to pay the going rate for the job. If you get four estimates from printers and one is half what the others are, don't give him the job. Choose one of the other three. Be sure to see their shop. If it's clean, their equipment is well maintained and there is evidence of pride in their workmanship, you'll probably get a first class product.

SOME EXAMPLES

The flagship of my Personal Promotion fleet is my Personal Brochure. It's done in Burgundy and White on a stiff cover material. Inside, my story is conveyed to the reader with a major emphasis on my credibility. At the same time, I'm presented in a very personable fashion. (See Sample at end of this chapter).

In addition to my Personal Brochure which is distributed far and wide, my other main handout is my "Things to Do" pad. It too is done in Burgundy and White. (See Sample at end of this chapter).

I also have a custom post card. It's also done in Burgundy and White. I use it for saying a quick "Thank You" to Realtors who show our listings and to anyone who for any reason deserves a "Thank You" or note. (See Sample at end of this chapter).

Besides the letters I send my clients with my two annual promotions, I use several other letters regularly for various purposes. These letters are stored on hand in my computer. The computer extracts the correct names automatically from our database, and inserts them into each letter as instructed. I've included the main ones here, with a description of their purpose. My Letterhead is also printed in Burgundy on Classic Laid bond with a full colour photo. (See Samples at end of this chapter).

Your Personal Promotion Program should be aimed at the world at large. Targeted audiences should include your clients, your peers, your local business press, your creditors, your friends, and everybody else. It should tell your story clearly, yet subtly. It should be neither offensive nor brash. It should be a first class presentation of what you really are!

My Personal Brochure has three folds and contains six panels. Featured below is a reproduction that shows the style. One panel of the brochure is reprinted on each of the next six pages.

SAMPLE: PANEL 1
PERSONAL BROCHURE

#1 REALTOR, REMAX OF WESTERN
CANADA 1984, 1986, 1987 and 1988.

#1 CALGARY MLS REALTOR
1984, 1986 and 1987.

ONE OF
NORTH AMERICA'S
LEADING REALTORS
CAN BE YOUR
REALTOR TOO!

SAMPLE: PANEL 2
PERSONAL BROCHURE

SOME OF MARILYN'S PROFESSIONAL ACHIEVEMENTS

1. #1 MLS Realtor, Calgary Real Estate Board, 1984, 1986, 1987 and #2 1985, 1988, 1989.

2. #1 Realtor, RE/MAX of Western Canada 1984, 1986, 1987, 1988 and #2, 1983, 1985, 1989.

3. #1 Female Realtor, Calgary Real Estate Board, 8th consecutive year.

4. #1 Realtor, RE/MAX Calgary South, 10th consecutive year.

5. #1 Female and #4 Realtor overall, RE/MAX International, 1985.

6. #4 Realtor, RE/MAX Canada and #8 Realtor RE/MAX International 1989 (over 28,000 realtors, Canada & U.S.A.)

7. Member, prestigious "Million Dollar Club", Calgary Real Estate Board.

8. Recipient, Calgary Real Estate Board "Award of Merit" 9th consecutive year.

9. Named #3 Realtor, All Companies in Canada by Real Estate Sales People Magazine, 1985.

10. Member, Very Exclusive RE/MAX International 100% Club. Awarded only to very top producers in RE/MAX International System.

11. Only Realtor from Western Canada inducted into RE/MAX International "Hall of Fame" as a charter Member (only 41 internationally).

12. Author, fast selling book, "CHAMPIONSHIP SELLING".

24 Successful Years in Real Estate Sales.

(403) 256-2037

SAMPLE: PANEL 3
PERSONAL BROCHURE

COMMENTS FROM MARILYN'S PEERS AND COMPETITORS

"From Ottawa, where I sell Real Estate, I refer clients to other Realtors all over Canada. None are happier than the clients I refer to Marilyn Jennings in Calgary. Invariably they thank me for introducing them to such a true professional."

Realtor — Ottawa, Ontario

"As the owner of a competing Real Estate Company, I have found Marilyn Jennings to be fair, ethical and a real professional in all her dealings with us." *Owner — Competing Real Estate Firm*

"Marilyn is always happy to share her 'Secrets of Success' with others in the Real Estate Profession. She's a real professional and a credit to the business." *Salesperson — Competitor Firm*

"I have been referring clients from Edmonton to Marilyn for several years. Without exception these clients have been handled in a truly professional manner and have become Marilyn's greatest fans."

Agent/Owner — Edmonton Real Estate Firm

"Marilyn is an inspiration to our sales people and I'm sure to all in the business. We need more like her." *Manager — Branch Office, Competitor Firm*

THE PRESS COMMENTS

Feb. 14/86, Calgary Herald, Business Section, Widely Read and Respected Business Writer, Charles Frank, Wrote the Following:

"In Calgary Real Estate circles, Marilyn Jennings is a legend in her own time. The 42 year-old Jennings has been the top ranked Female Real Estate Agent with the Calgary Real Estate Board for the last four years. In 1984 she was the Board's Top Performer male or female. In 1985, her sales commissions alone topped the $500,000 mark."

Names available on request.

(403) 256-2037

SAMPLE: PANEL 4
PERSONAL BROCHURE

COMMENTS FROM MARILYN'S CLIENTS

"Marilyn Jennings has listed and sold numerous properties for us in a truly impressive and professional manner. We recommend her highly."
Manager — Trust Company

"When you are not in the business world every day, you don't decide to sell your home and buy another one without being concerned. When we met Marilyn Jennings, our concerns turned to confidence. She'll always be our Realtor."
Ironworker — Calgary

"I call on Marilyn Jennings on a regular basis for professional Real Estate advice. She knows the market. She's in tune with current trends. I recommend her to my clients frequently. They are always impressed." *Senior Partner — Law Firm*

"Our two previous Real Estate experiences were both disasters. It wasn't until we listed our home and purchased another through Marilyn Jennings that we realized how smoothly Real Estate transactions should go. She's everything a Realtor should be!" *Welder — Calgary*

"If everyone thinking of listing or buying a home had the opportunity of choosing Marilyn Jennings as their Realtor there would be a lot more satisfied sellers and buyers out there. What a difference being a professional makes."
Rancher — DeWinton

"Marilyn Jennings is successful. She has experience and credibility. She markets properties for us on a regular basis because she gets the job done right."
Banker — Calgary

"Marilyn Jennings is our Realtor because she cared about us before, during and since our real estate deal. She's a real pro with a lot of class — a real genuine person who really knows her business."
Chief of Security — Calgary Firm

"We felt so comfortable and at ease with Marilyn Jennings. She did everything in our best interest. She has our total loyalty and respect and we refer everyone we meet to her."
Oil Field Consultant and Accountant — Calgary

Names available on request.

(403) 256-2037

SAMPLE: PANEL 5
PERSONAL BROCHURE

COMMENTS FROM MARILYN'S EMPLOYERS AND FELLOW EMPLOYEES

"Of the more than 24,000 RE/MAX Realtors internationally, only the very top producers and earners achieve membership in our Very Exclusive 100% Club. One name that is there consistently, year after year, is that of Marilyn Jennings. We congratulate her once again for a great year in 1988 and know she will be "Above the Crowd" again in 1989."

Gail Lininger — President
RE/MAX ® INTERNATIONAL INC.

"Marilyn Jennings is the only Charter Member to be inducted into the RE/MAX International "HALL OF FAME" from Western Canada. That's an incredible achievement but not surprising because her professional approach and consideration for her clients make her one of the very best in the business."

Robert H. Cherot — Regional Director
RE/MAX ® of Western Canada

"Marilyn Jennings is consistently the top Realtor in our office and always among the very top Realtors on the Calgary Real Estate Board. She has the respect of all those who work with her and we are proud to have such a successful professional on our winning team."   *Rick Baker — President*
RE/MAX ® Real Estate Calgary South Ltd.

"Whenever I need a bit of advice or assistance with a Real Estate matter, I call on Marilyn Jennings. As busy as she is, she always finds time to help. I'm glad Marilyn is in our office and not some other one."   *Fellow Realtor —* **RE/MAX** ® South

"Marilyn Jennings has been a real inspiration to me. Her enthusiasm, her high standards and her professional way of doing things have taught me much about how to be more successful."
Fellow Realtor — **RE/MAX** ® South

"The secretaries at her office admire and respect Marilyn. She is always appreciative and easy to get along with. She has excellent rapport with Staff, Realtors, Lawyers and Her Clients. We get nothing but praise for Marilyn. She never complains, and is a real pleasure to work with."

Jane Frohlick — Conveyancing Secretary
RE/MAX ® Real Estate South

(403) 256-2037

SAMPLE: PANEL 6
PERSONAL BROCHURE

EXPERIENCE + RESPECT + CONFIDENCE = CREDIBILITY AND PERFORMANCE

MARILYN JENNINGS HAS:

- 24 YEARS OF SUCCESSFUL REAL ESTATE LISTING AND SELLING EXPERIENCE.

- THE RESPECT AND ADMIRATION OF HER PEERS **AND** COMPETITORS IN THE REAL ESTATE PROFESSION.

- THE CONFIDENCE OF HER CLIENTS.

- THE UNQUALIFIED SUPPORT OF HER COMPANY LOCALLY, NATIONALLY AND INTERNATIONALLY.

- AN ENVIABLE RECORD OF ACHIEVEMENT AND PERFORMANCE IN THE REAL ESTATE PROFESSION.

MARILYN HAS THE CREDIBILITY TO BE YOUR REALTOR TOO!! CALL HER TODAY AT

TEL. **(403) 256-2037**

FAX **(403) 256-1249**

CAR **(403) 540-8988**

REPRESENTING:
RE/MAX ® REAL ESTATE CALGARY SOUTH LTD.

This pamphlet not intended to solicit properties already listed with other realtors.

SAMPLE:
THINGS TO
DO PAD

THINGS TO DO **TODAY**

Date_____	Completed
1_____	☐
2_____	☐
3_____	☐
4_____	☐
5_____	☐
6_____	☐
7_____	☐
8_____	☐
9_____	☐
10_____	☐
11_____	☐
12 Phone **MARILYN** to buy or sell property.	☐

MARILYN JENNINGS
representing

RE/MAX real estate south
(MLS Realtor)

(403)-278-5256

"25 Years in Real Estate Sales"

SAMPLE: CUSTOM POST CARD
USED TO THANK REALTORS FOR
SHOWING MY LISTINGS AND TO SAY
"THANK YOU" OR "CONGRATULATIONS"
TO ANY DESERVING INDIVIDUAL

#1 REALTOR, REMAX OF
WESTERN CANADA
1984, 1986, 1987 and 1988.

#1 CALGARY MLS REALTOR
1984, 1986 and 1987.

Return To: P.O. Box 8425, Stn. 'F'
Calgary, Alberta T2J 2V5

STAMP

TO:

REPRESENTING: REMAX REAL ESTATE CALGARY SOUTH LTD. PH: 256-2037

December 19, 1989

Peter Gurr
1234 58 Street SW
Calgary, AB
T2T 1T1

Dear Peter:

In a few short weeks another year -- 1989 -- as well as another decade -- the 1980's -- will have come and gone. It's hard to believe, but some of you have been dealing with me for over 10 years now. Valued clients like you have made the 80's a memorable decade for me, so I want to say a sincere "thank you" for that. And I also want to thank you for making 1989 the best year I've ever had in Real Estate. I sincerely hope the accompanying gift helps make your Holiday Season a bit more enjoyable, and, in a small way allows you to share in the excitement and success you helped me achieve in 1989.

I'm presently spending my spare time revising and updating my book "Championship Selling" so it can be reprinted early in 1990. It's been a "Best Seller" since 1987 and demand continues to increase each year as it becomes better known in the Real Estate Industry. It presently sells in the U.S.A., Great Britain, Australia, New Zealand, and South Africa in addition to Canada.

By years end I'll have participated in over 200 client transactions. The best I've ever done in a single year before was 184 transactions. Although it's too early to tell where I'll end up in the overall statistics for 1989, it's possible I could be #1 for both the Calgary Real Estate Board and Re/Max of Western Canada again. If I don't make the #1 spot for the Calgary Real Estate Board at least the honour will stay in the family. My son-in-law will be the one who wins the honour if I don't. In any case I've been either #1 or #2 for the Calgary Real Estate Board for the past 6 years. As for Re/Max of Western Canada, I'm involved in a real close race this year. I could end up losing the #1 spot after holding it for the past 3

"25 Years in Real Estate Sales"
MARILYN JENNINGS

**#1 REALTOR, REMAX OF
WESTERN CANADA**
1984, 1986, 1987, 1988 and
#2, 1983, 1985 and 1989.

#1 calgary MLS REALTOR
1984, 1986, 1987 and
#2, 1985, 1988 and 1989.

TEL. (403) 256-2037
FAX. (403) 256-1249
CAR (403) 540-8988

representing

RE/MAX real estate calgary
south ltd

p.o. box 8425
station "f"
calgary, alberta T2J 2V5

years. I've been #1 for Re/Max of Western Canada 4 out of the past 5 years and #2 on 3 occasions during the past 7 years.

Once again, over 85% of my business has come from clients who dealt with me previously and from others who've been referred to me. Because of your continued support I've been able to rise to the top of my profession and stay there. And I want you to know that I really, really appreciate it!

1989 has been a record year for the Real Estate industry in Calgary. As of November 21, 1989 the Calgary Real Estate Board broke the $2 Billion dollar mark for the first time in history. A new record for the number of Housing Units sold in a calendar year has also been established. New Homes are being built and sold at an ever increasing pace. Our population is on the upswing. More and more companies are transferring employees here. Calgary is among the more desirable destinations for employees who are given a choice of locations to transfer to. That's because of our buoyant economy and the excellent housing values here compared to elsewhere.

The present market in Calgary is ideal. Sales are brisk. Interest rates are stable and reasonable. Price levels are fair to both buyers and sellers. There's a good supply of homes in nearly all price ranges in most areas of the city and surrounding environs, although the supply of listings has been shrinking steadily in recent months. In general, I expect these trends to continue and the market to remain strong in 1990. During the first half of the year I experienced experience moderate price increases. However, towards the end of 1990, depending on how the proposed Goods and Services Tax finally impacts Real Estate sales in Canada, we could experience significant tightening in our market.

Before I close I'd like to ask the same favour I asked of everyone in my letter last June. I need your help. Please tell everyone you know that a favourite line used by my competitors when competing with me for business, just isn't so. Prospective clients are often told that I only list and sell expensive larger homes. As you know, nothing could be further from the truth. I list and sell homes in every price range and in all parts of the city and surrounding areas. Every client is equally important to me! This year I've listed and sold properties that ranged in value from $29,000 to over $2,000,000. However, the vast majority of my listings and sales fall into the $80,000 to $200,000 price range. Many of my new clients are sons and daughters of long time clients and are buying their first home. They'll be purchasing bigger homes as they grow older just as their parents have done. So as far as I'm concerned the client who buys an inexpensive starter home from me today, is the same client who will list it with me and buy a more expensive home from me tomorrow. I list and sell properties in all price ranges, so I can accommodate all members of the families who deal with me, as well as their friends.

So, if I can be of assistance at any time to you, your friends, associates, acquaintances or relatives please call, no matter how large or small the need may be.

And do have a Blessed and Holy Christmas and a Happy and Prosperous 1990.

Your Realtor,

Marilyn Jennings

SAMPLE: FOLLOW-UP
TO MARKET ANALYSIS
LETTER

January 1, 1991

Peter Gurr
1234 - 58 Street
Calgary, AB
T2T 1T1

Dear Peter:

Thank you for meeting with me and allowing me the privilege of doing a "Market Analysis" for you.

Should you decide to sell, I will be pleased to handle the sale of your home for you and, more importantly, have you as one of my valued clients.

If however, you decide not to sell, please call and let me know. In that case, I would be happy to provide you with regular computer updates on the market.

If I can be of service to you again, or to your friends, relatives, or acquaintances, please call me at any time.

Your Realtor,

Marilyn Jennings.

"25 Years in Real Estate Sales"
MARILYN JENNINGS

#1 REALTOR, REMAX OF WESTERN CANADA
1984, 1986, 1987, 1988 and #2, 1983, 1985 and 1989.

#1 calgary MLS REALTOR
1984, 1986, 1987 and #2, 1985, 1988 and 1989.

TEL. (403) 256-2037
FAX. (403) 256-1249
CAR (403) 540-8988

representing

RE/MAX real estate calgary
south ltd.
p.o. box 8425
station "f"
calgary, alberta T2J 2V5

SAMPLE: LETTER TO CLIENT REFERRED TO ME BY REALTOR OR OTHER SOURCE

January 15, 1991

Peter Gurr
-234 58 Street
Anycity, Anywhere
S16 1X5

Dear Peter:

It's a pleasure to enclose some information about the Real Estate Market in Calgary. I have also enclosed some information about myself for your perusal and to serve as an introduction to you.

If there is anything else that I can do or send you before you come to Calgary to look at houses, please write to me at the address below or phone me at (403) 256-2037 and I will be happy to oblige.

I am eagerly looking forward to meeting you, working with you and, far more important, to having you as one of my valued clients.

In the meantime I remain,

Your Realtor,

Marilyn Jennings.
Enclosures.

"25 Years in Real Estate Sales"
MARILYN JENNINGS

#1 REALTOR, REMAX OF WESTERN CANADA
1984, 1986, 1987, 1988 and
#2, 1983, 1985 and 1989.

#1 calgary MLS REALTOR
1984, 1986, 1987 and
#2, 1985, 1988 and 1989.

TEL. (403) 256-2037
FAX. (403) 256-1249
CAR (403) 540-8988

representing

RE/MAX real estate calgary
south ltd.

p.o. box 8425
station "f"
calgary, alberta T2J 2V5

SAMPLE: LETTER TO CLIENT
OR OTHER CONTACT REFERRING
ANOTHER CLIENT TO ME

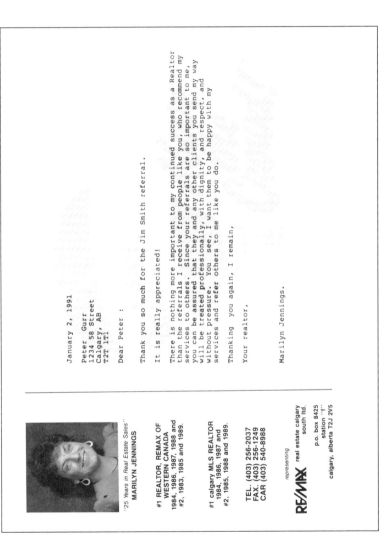

January 2, 1991

Peter Gurr
1234 58 Street
Calgary, AB
T2T 1T1

Dear Peter :

Thank you so much for the Jim Smith referral.

It is really appreciated!

There is nothing more important to my continued success as a Realtor than the referrals I receive from people like you, who recommend my services to others. Since your referrals are so important to me, you can be assured that they and any other clients you send my way will be treated professionally, with dignity, and respect, and without pressure. You see, I want them to be happy with my services and refer others to me like you do.

Thanking you again, I remain,

Your realtor,

Marilyn Jennings.

"25 Years in Real Estate Sales"
MARILYN JENNINGS

#1 REALTOR, REMAX OF
WESTERN CANADA
1984, 1986, 1987, 1988 and
#2, 1983, 1985 and 1989.

#1 calgary MLS REALTOR
1984, 1986, 1987 and
#2, 1985, 1988 and 1989.

TEL. (403) 256-2037
FAX. (403) 256-1249
CAR (403) 540-8988

representing

RE/MAX real estate calgary
south ltd.
p.o. box 8425
station "f"
calgary, alberta T2J 2V5

226 *Championship Selling*

SAMPLE: LETTER TO REALTOR REFERRING CLIENT TO ME

January 2, 1991

John Smith
Re/Max Realty
1234 56 Street
Edmonton, AB
T5T 1T1

Dear John:

Thank you so much for the Jim Smith referral. It is really appreciated! Rest assured it will be handled expeditiously and professionally. When the referral forms arrive from your office I will execute and return them to you immediately. I will personally see that your referral fee is sent immediately upon receipt of the commission by our office.

If there is anything further I should know or do, please advise me by letter at the address below or phone me at (403) 256-2037.

Thanking you again, I remain,

Yours truly,

Marilyn Jennings.

"25 Years in Real Estate Sales"
MARILYN JENNINGS

#1 REALTOR, REMAX OF WESTERN CANADA
1984, 1986, 1987, 1988 and #2, 1983, 1985 and 1989.

#1 calgary MLS REALTOR 1984, 1986, 1987 and #2, 1985, 1988 and 1989.

TEL. (403) 256-2037
FAX. (403) 256-1249
CAR (403) 540-8988

representing

RE/MAX real estate calgary south ltd.

p.o. box 8425
station "f"
calgary, alberta T2J 2V5

SAMPLE: LETTER TO REALTOR
TO WHOM I HAVE REFERRED
A CLIENT

January 1, 1991

John Smith
Re/Max Realty
1234 56 Street
Edmonton, AB
T5T 1T1

Dear John:

It's a pleasure for me to enclose the appropriate forms regarding the Jim Smith referral we spoke about by phone. Please sign and return them to me as soon as possible.

Knowing you will conclude a transaction with this client, please ensure that a 25% referral fee is sent to RE/MAX REAL ESTATE SOUTH, SUITE 390, 11012 MACLEOD TRAIL SOUTH, CALGARY, ALBERTA, T2J 6A5, upon receipt of the commission by your office.

Kindly keep me apprised of your progress.

Should I become aware of anything else you should be aware of, I will contact you immediately.

Wishing you continued success, I remain,

Yours truly,

Marilyn Jennings.

"25 Years in Real Estate Sales"
MARILYN JENNINGS

#1 REALTOR, REMAX OF WESTERN CANADA
1984, 1986, 1987, 1988 and #2, 1983, 1985 and 1989.

#1 calgary MLS REALTOR
1984, 1986, 1987 and #2, 1985, 1988 and 1989.

TEL. (403) 256-2037
FAX. (403) 256-1249
CAR (403) 540-8988

representing

RE/MAX real estate calgary south ltd.
p.o. box 8425
station "f"
calgary, alberta T2J 2V5

SAMPLE: LETTER TO CLIENT
AFTER TRANSACTION HAS CLOSED

January 2, 1991

Peter Gurr
Anycompany
1234 58 Street SW
Calgary, AB
T2T 1T1

Dear Dear Peter::

Thank you for allowing me to be of service in your recent Real Estate transaction.

It was truly a pleasure dealing with you and more importantly having you as a valued client.

There is nothing more important to my continued success as a Realtor than the referrals I receive from previous clients like you.

I've enclosed a few of my personal brochures in case any of your fellow employees, relatives, friends, or acquaintances need assistance in a Real Estate matter in the future. You can be sure that anyone you send my way will be treated professionally, with dignity, and respect and without pressure. You see, I want them to be happy with my services and refer others to me as well.

Thanking you again, I remain

Your Realtor,

Marilyn Jennings
Enclosures

"25 Years in Real Estate Sales"
MARILYN JENNINGS

**#1 REALTOR, REMAX OF
WESTERN CANADA**
1984, 1986, 1987, 1988 and
#2, 1983, 1985 and 1989.

#1 calgary MLS REALTOR
1984, 1986, 1987 and
#2, 1985, 1988 and 1989.

TEL. (403) 256-2037
FAX. (403) 256-1249
CAR (403) 540-8988

representing

RE/MAX real estate calgary
south ltd.

p.o. box 8425
station "f"
calgary, alberta T2J 2V5

SAMPLE: LETTER TO PERSON WHO HAS REFERRED CLIENT TO ME. SENT AFTER TRANSACTION HAS BEEN CONCLUDED WITH CLIENT

January 2, 1991

Peter Gurr
1234 58 Street
Calgary, AB
T2T 1T1

Dear Peter :

Some time ago you referred Jim Smith to me. In the meantime I listed and we recently concluded a sale with them!

Once more, I want to say how much I appreciate the referrals you send my way. Again I want to assure you that all those you refer to me will be treated professionally with dignity and respect and without pressure. I look forward to hearing from you again in the near future.

Thanking you again, I remain,

Your realtor,

Marilyn Jennings

"25 Years in Real Estate Sales"
MARILYN JENNINGS

#1 REALTOR, REMAX OF WESTERN CANADA
1984, 1986, 1987, 1988 and #2, 1983, 1985 and 1989.

#1 calgary MLS REALTOR
1984, 1986, 1987 and #2, 1985, 1988 and 1989.

TEL. (403) 256-2037
FAX. (403) 256-1249
CAR (403) 540-8988

representing

RE/MAX real estate calgary south ltd.
p.o. box 8425 station "f"
calgary, alberta T2J 2V5

" C H A P T E R   31 "

CLOSING
THOUGHTS

Well folks, that's just about it! I'd like to leave you

with these few key thoughts:

Systems Give Life To Plans!! Every salesperson needs a system to bring his/her plans to life!

Remember, you can never be "ABOVE AVERAGE" as long as you pursue "AVERAGE" goals.

When you set out to pursue "ABOVE AVERAGE" goals, most people in your office and in the industry, will be unable to relate to what you are doing. Don't let this upset you. Just remember that they, like you, were hired and trained by "AVERAGE" Managers to think, act, work, and set goals like "AVERAGE" Realtors.

Remember also, that if you set goals for yourself and you work hard to achieve them, you're going to get lucky. LUCK IS A BY-PRODUCT OF ACHIEVING A GOAL!

As commission salespeople we're in business for ourselves. We have to be concerned about building our businesses. Worked faithfully,"An Effective Client Retention Program" together with "An Active Referral System", can provide a salesperson in any field, with an almost limitless supply of clients after a short number of years. At the same time the quality of clientele, he or she works with, will be continually upgraded.

There are Negative Time Wasters such as "resident economists", "office politicians" and "social gadflys" in nearly every office. If you're going to be successful you can't afford to associate with negative people who waste your time. You have to distance yourself sufficiently from these and other types who do not make a positive contribution to your success. Otherwise they'll become a catalyst for your failure.

Learn to become a consistent Good Lister. Good listers never find themselves in a "Slump". They're "SLUMP PROOF". Having more listings is the "cure" for virtually every problem the market can place in the way of a Realtor. When you become a consistent Good Lister, provided you apply the three distinct elements of the Championship Selling System (see Chapter 2), you can literally guarantee yourself any income you want to earn, selling Real Estate.

Get to know or develop statistics for your area. You can then make adjustments to keep the "law of averages" on your side as Market conditions change. Life need not be a gamble. You can win consistently — but only if the odds are in your favor.

You can increase your sales if you critically analyze the management of your time. Concentrate your efforts on spending your time with the people who are going to buy your product. Let others tidy up the loose ends. Make sure that your time, and the time of your employees, is spent generating the best quality prospects, in sufficient quantity to keep you booked two to three weeks in advance at all times.

Time management means more than squeezing extra sales calls into a given period of time. It means spending your time doing the most productive tasks, at the right time, as Efficiently and Effectively as possible, while delegating the unproductive tasks to others, so you can attain your goals.

When you hit the "Time Barrier" it's time to hire an assistant. You can delegate all the unproductive tasks to your assistant allowing you to concentrate on income producing activities.

Always remember the "Delegation Rule". If it can be done by someone for less than you're worth per hour it should be delegated to someone else unless there is a compelling reason for not doing so. Exceptions to this rule should be few and far between.

You and your employees need all the essential tools of the trade to be successful. Don't lose $1000 trying to save $100 that should be spent on catalogues or samples.

Never underestimate the value of leisure time. To remain sharp, physically and mentally alert, you have to take time off and relax! Everyone functions best when they are rested and recharged.

Be sure your Personal Promotion material and Personal Promotion projects always have a classy touch. Go First Class And Be Consistent. And don't forget that quality is more important than quantity.

Remember, it takes no more time or effort to aim high in life than it does to aim low — to demand abundance rather than accept poverty. This truth came to my attention over 30 years ago, when I first read my favorite book "Think and Grow Rich" by Napoleon Hill. A poem in that same book illustrates its meaning much better than anything I could say.

Now, I'd like to leave you with that poem, and dedicate it especially to those in our profession who cut commission on every deal, and work for a fraction of what we're worth. This problem, whether we realize it or not, is the main reason many Realtors fail to succeed. I have to contend with it all the time the same as many of you. In 25 years in the business I've never found it necessary to cut commission. This poem tells why. It goes like this:

> I bargained with life for a penny
> And life would pay no more,
> However, I begged at evening
> When I counted my scanty store.
>
> For life is a just employer,
> He gives you what you ask
> But once you have set the wages,
> Why, you must bear the task.
>
> I worked for a menial's hire,
> Only to learn, dismayed,
> That any wage I had asked of life,
> Life would have willingly paid.

Good Luck And Good Selling!!